The First Souvenirs
Enamelled Vessels from Hadrian's Wall

Edited by David J. Breeze

With Contributions

by

Lindsay Allason-Jones, Paul Holder, Fraser Hunter,
Ralph Jackson, Ernst Künzl, Noel Maheo and Sally Worrell

To the memory of Brian Dobson
(13 September 1931 - 19 July 2012)

and to celebrate the birth of

Connie Catherine Breeze born 27 April 2011
Edward Laurence Tom Pearce born 2 April 2011

The First Souvenirs Enamelled Vessels from Hadrian's Wall

Edited by

David J. Breeze

With Contributions

by

Lindsay Allason-Jones, Paul Holder, Fraser Hunter,
Ralph Jackson, Ernst Künzl, Noel Maheo and Sally Worrell

CUMBERLAND AND WESTMORLAND
ANTIQUARIAN AND ARCHAEOLOGICAL SOCIETY
2012

Cumberland and Westmorland
Antiquarian and Archaeological Society
Hon. General Editor
Dr Jean Turnbull

The First Souvenirs
Enamelled vessels from Hadrian's Wall

Edited by David J. Breeze

EXTRA SERIES NO. XXXVII
On behalf of the Organising Committee of the Pilgrimage of Hadrian's Wall 2009

ISBN 978 1 873124 58 1

Printed by
Titus Wilson & Son, Kendal
2012

Contents

Organising Committee for the
Thirteenth Pilgrimage of Hadrian's Wall

Lindsay Allason-Jones
Paul Austen
Paul Bidwell
David Breeze (Chairman)
Ian Caruana (Treasurer)
Jim Crow
Bill Griffiths (Secretary)
Richard Hingley
Nick Hodgson
Rachel Newman
Pete Wilson

Preface

The first Pilgrimage of Hadrian's Wall was held in 1849 and was led by John Collingwood Bruce, a Newcastle historian, schoolmaster and Nonconformist Minister. It was attended by about 24 people. The second Pilgrimage did not occur until 1886, but they have been held every ten years since, with the exception of the War years (Edwards and Breeze 2000 lists the Pilgrimages and relevant publications).

The 13th Pilgrimage was organised, as usual, by the Society of Antiquaries of Newcastle upon Tyne and the Cumberland and Westmorland Antiquarian and Archaeological Society and was held from 8 to 14 August 2009. It was attended by over 220 people, each provided with a handbook compiled by Nick Hodgson (2009).

The primary aim of the Pilgrimage is to consider new work on Hadrian's Wall. Accordingly, military remains were inspected from the fort at Moresby on the Cumbrian coast to that at South Shields at the mouth of the River Tyne, and special exhibitions were mounted. One of the spectacular new discoveries of the last ten years is the Ilam Pan, sometimes called the Staffordshire Moorlands Pan, found by a metal detectorist in 2003. Ernst Künzl, the foremost expert on Roman enamelled vessels, was invited to attend the Pilgrimage and deliver a lecture placing the new discovery in its setting. Tullie House Museum, Carlisle, also prepared a special exhibition containing the Rudge Cup, Amiens Patera and Ilam Pan to coincide with the Pilgrimage; these vessels had only once previously been displayed together, at the 2008 Hadrian exhibition at the British Museum.

The lecture delivered by Ernst Künzl at Carlisle on 9 August 2009 is the genesis of this publication. It is reproduced here, expanded and enlarged, together with papers on the Rudge Cup by Lindsay Allason-Jones and on the Ilam Pan by Ralph Jackson, both originally given at the seminar on the Ilam Pan at the British Museum in 2005, and a report on the Amiens Patera by Noel Maheo. Lindsay Allason-Jones has also prepared a report on the Hildburgh Fragment. The papers on the individual vessels are accompanied by a review of the place-names which appear on them by Paul Holder. Two further papers extend the range of this review, a report by Sally Worrell on similar material reported through the Portable Antiquities Scheme and a review of similar vessels from the frontier zone in Britain by Fraser Hunter. Descriptions of these pans and similar vessels from Britain are provided at the beginning of this booklet with some conclusions at the end. There is inevitably some overlap between the various contributors, nor do they all offer the same conclusions. It has seemed sensible to retain this element of overlap in view of the necessity for each contributor to place their item(s) in context and argue their own case while bearing in mind that certainty in such matters cannot be possible.

David J. Breeze
Chairman, 2009 Pilgrimage of Hadrian's Wall

List of Contributors

LINDSAY ALLASON-JONES
President of the Society of Antiquaries of Newcastle upon Tyne

DAVID J. BREEZE
President of the Cumberland and Westmorland Antiquarian and
Archaeological Society

PAUL HOLDER
The University of Manchester Library

FRASER HUNTER
Iron Age and Roman Curator, National Museums of Scotland

RALPH JACKSON
Curator of Romano-British Collections, The British Museum

ERNST KÜNZL
Former director of the Römisch-Germanisches Zentralmuseum, Mainz

NOEL MAHEO
Curator, Museum of Picardy, Amiens

SALLY WORRELL
Prehistoric and Roman Finds Advisor, Portable Antiquities Scheme

List of Figures

List of Tables

Editor's Notes

The 'pans' are about the size of ladles, and, as each may have been provided with a handle, may have served such a purpose. They have been variously termed pan, skillet or cup, or by a Roman name, *patera or trulla*. The word skillet, defined by the Concise Oxford Dictionary as a 'small metal pot with long handle & usu(ally) legs used in cooking', perhaps comes close to being the most appropriate word, though none of the surviving Roman vessels is known to have had legs. Accordingly, Ralph Jackson has recommended the use of a more neutral term such as a 'small handled pan' or 'small pan'. In this publication, the vessels are referred to by the generic name 'pan', though the traditional name for each vessel is retained. A catalogue of the pans relating to Hadrian's Wall is provided at the beginning of this book (chapter 1).

ABBREVIATIONS

AE	*L'Année Epigraphique*
CIL	*Corpus Inscriptionum Latinarum*
RIB	*The Roman Inscriptions of Britain*

ACKNOWLEDGEMENTS

We are grateful to all those who have kindly supplied illustrations for reproduction: Bad Pyrmont, Museum (2.6); The British Museum (2.1, 2.2, 2.5, 2.8, 5.1-5.9); Cambridge University Museum of Archaeology and Anthropology (9.8); CFA Archaeology (9.3); Council for British Archaeology and Chris Evans (9.4); the Kunsthistorisches Museum, Vienna (2.3); North Lincolnshire Museum (8.1, photograph by L. Staves); Norfolk Museums and Archaeology Service (9.10); Oxford University Press (9.9); Museum of Picardy (4.3); Portable Antiquities Scheme (8.1-8.17); Rheinisches Landesmuseum, Bonn (2.7); Roman Baths Museum, Bath, courtesy of Stephen Clews (1.5 and 5.10); Römisch-Germanisches Zentralmuseum Mainz (2.9, 2.10 and 2.11 courtesy of Barbara Pferdehirt; 2.11 and 2.13 courtesy of Julia Ribbeck and Guido Heinz); The Society of Antiquaries of Newcastle upon Tyne (6.3 and 9.4); The Trustees of the National Museums of Scotland (9.1); Tullie House Museum, Carlisle for permission to use the photographs of the vessels taken while they were in the museum in 2009 (1.1-1.3, 3.1, 4.1, 4.2); The Victoria and Albert Museum (1.4, 6.1 and 6.2). 5.6 is by Saul Peckham and Stephen Crummy. 9.2, 9.3 and 9.5 are drawn by Alan Braby. The editor is also grateful to David Clarke and Tim Padley of Tullie House Museum and to Ralph Jackson of the British Museum for help with the illustrations. Ernst Künzl would like to thank Ralph Jackson (London), Catherine Johns (London), Constantin Künzl (Heidelberg/D) and Barbara Pferdehirt (Mainz/D). The coloured drawings of the fragment from Spain (2.13) and the jug and the *patera* in the Römisch-Germanisches Zentralmuseum Mainz (2.11) were created by Julia Ribbeck (Mainz/D) and Guido Heinz (Mainz/D). Lindsay Allason-

Jones wishes to thank His Grace the Duke of Northumberland and the staff at Alnwick Castle for granting access to the Rudge Cup. Lindsay Allason-Jones, David Breeze and Paul Holder are also grateful to Paul Wilkinson and Rosie Mills at the Victoria and Albert Museum for tracing the Hildburgh Fragment and allowing them research access to the item. Ralph Jackson thanks Deborah Klemperer and Kevin Blackburn for showing him the findspot of the Ilam Pan and discussing its finding circumstances, and Noel Maheo and François Vasselle for providing details of the discovery and context of the Amiens Patera. Fraser Hunter would like to thank Ralph Jackson for the chance to examine the Ilam Pan and other items in the British Museum, Jacek Andrzejowski for information on the Jartypory find, Hilary Cool for pointing him towards the hexagonal flasks, Jack Hunter and David Devereux for information on John Nicholson, Chris Chippindale and Imogen Gunn for information on the Great Chesterford fragment, and Liz Elmore for information on a find from Hockwold-cum-Wilton. The editor is particularly grateful to Lindsay Allason-Jones for her considerable help with the copy editing and advice throughout.

Summary

Three small decorated vessels bearing the names of forts along the western sector of Hadrian's Wall from Bowness-on-Solway to Great Chesters have been found, two in central and southern England, the third in France. The Ilam Pan bears a free-flowing Celtic-style decoration with the letters cut into the vessel. The Rudge Cup and the Amiens Patera have a geometric pattern believed to represent Hadrian's Wall – the same design appears on the Hildburgh Fragment (probably a flask) and the Bath Pan – but otherwise bear slightly different decorations. On both the Rudge Cup and the Amiens Patera the fort names are in relief and therefore form part of the cast. The incision of the letters on the Ilam Pan indicates that it was made as a general purpose object and later personalised. The Ilam Pan includes the name Draco and probably the name of Hadrian's Wall, *vallum Aelium*. All bowls were once enamelled; the Amiens Patera was found with a handle, also enamelled. Re-examination of the vessels cast doubt on some of the earlier identification of the colours.

Ernst Künzl argues that the vessels were made in Britain. Lindsay Allason-Jones suggests that the similarity between the Rudge Cup, the Amiens Skillet and the Hildburgh Fragment indicates that the vessels may have been made in the same workshop, and, in view of the fact that the different fort names on the vessels suggests local knowledge, that this workshop lay close to the Wall; Carlisle is the favoured location.

Paul Holder suggests that the particular names on the Ilam Pan imply a date in the reign of Hadrian for its manufacture, while Lindsay Allason-Jones argues for a Hadrianic date for the Rudge Cup. Ernst Künzl suggests that all three pans were probably made following the return to Hadrian's Wall from the Antonine Wall in the 160s, the rebuilding of the western sector of the Wall in stone presenting an appropriate occasion for the production of such vessels.

All three vessels bearing the names of forts would appear to have been souvenirs of Hadrian's Wall. This interpretation is reinforced by the discovery of all five vessels away from Hadrian's Wall. They reflect, Ernst Künzl proposes, the contemporary appreciation that Hadrian's Wall was a special frontier. There are strong arguments for the Ilam Pan being the earliest, made as a general item and personalised for Draco; in this case the other vessels may have been created following a realisation that there was a market for such items. As souvenirs, they may have had no other function. A link to wine-drinking, perhaps by veterans of the Roman army, has been suggested. The discovery of several pans on high-status sites may not be coincidental. Ralph Jackson draws attention to the relationship of several pans to water and suggests a ritual association.

Fraser Hunter and Ralph Jackson discuss the antecedents of the styles of decoration on the pans and related vessels, the former emphasising the role of the eclectic nature of frontier society in the creation of these designs. Hunter also acknowledges the value placed on these vessels by people living beyond the frontier, those to the north-west of the Empire preferring pans and related 'open' vessels while those to the east had more diverse tastes.

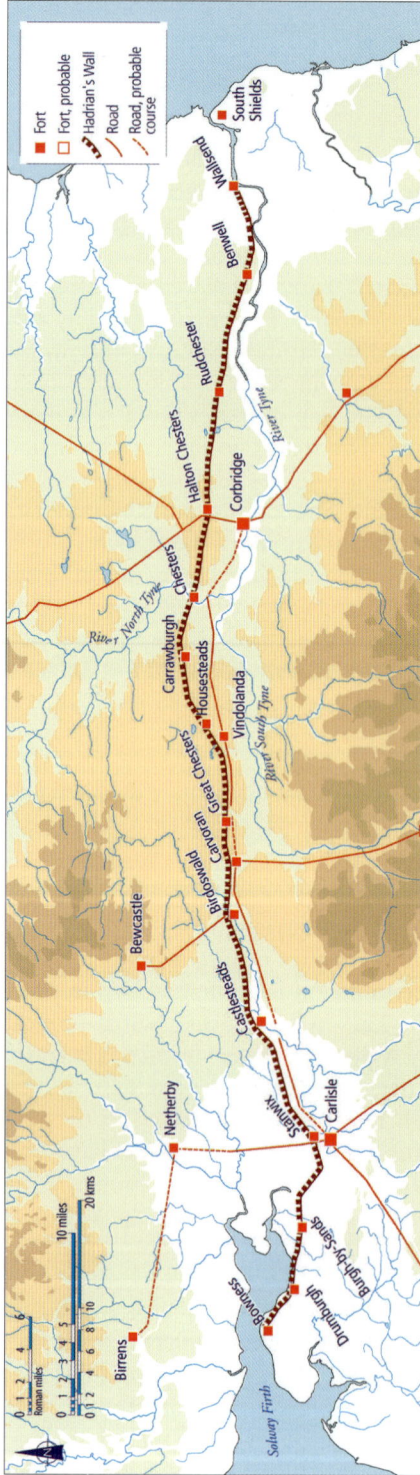

Map of Hadrian's Wall

Chapter 1
Catalogue of the British Pans

David J. Breeze

This is a list of the pans either found in Britain or relating to Britain which are most relevant to the Hadrian's Wall Series. The three bearing the names of forts on Hadrian's Wall are listed in order of discovery.

Rudge Cup (*RIB* II. 2, 2415.53; Bruce 1880, 139-41; Cowen and Richmond 1935)

Found in 1725 in a well at a possible Roman villa at Rudge Coppice near Froxfield, Wiltshire. Now in Alnwick Castle, Northumberland.

Figure 1.1. The Rudge Cup

A bronze bowl. Diameter at rim 89-93mm; diameter at base 58mm; height 46mm. Decorated in a geometric pattern. At the base of the pan are two rows of squares. Above this are alternating squares and crescents. The large squares are divided into four small squares with three 'crenellations' at the top and two crescents at the bottom. In between are two large crescents placed back-to-back, each containing a large dot or small circle, and two smaller crescents. Red, green or white and possibly blue enamel. A hole in the side of the vessel may indicate the former position of a handle. Horsley (1732, 329) recorded the existence of a detached base, now lost.

The letters are moulded in relief below the rim. Letter height 5mm. There are serifs on the letters and the As are blind, that is they have no central bar. The text comprises 36 letters:

.A.MAIS ABALLAVA VXELODVM CAMBOGLANS BANNA

There are two interpuncts either side of an A which does not seem to be part of a word. This would seem to indicate the starting point of the inscription. 'A' is therefore the opening preposition to the list of names. These are the names of the forts at the western end of Hadrian's Wall in the correct order, reading from west to east: Bowness-on-Solway, Burgh-by-Sands, Stanwix, Castlesteads and Birdoswald.

Amiens Patera (*AE* 1950, 56; Vasselle 1949-50; Heurgon 1951; Heurgon 1952a; Bayard and Massy 1983, 148-149, fig. 67; Trésors archéologiques du Nord de la France 1997, 77 no. 82)

Found in 1949 in a Roman house in Amiens. Now in the Musée de Picardie, Amiens.

A bronze *patera*. Diameter at rim 100mm; height 56mm. Decorated in a geometric pattern. There are two rows of squares at the bottom. Above there is an alternating pattern. One element consists of squares with two crescents below, surmounted by 'crenellations', the other of two crescents, each containing two small circles or dots and with another circle or dot above and below. Red, blue and green enamel.

Figure 1.2. The Amiens Patera

The handle, 90mm long, was found separated from the bowl, its breaking off causing slight damage to the vessel; it has since been attached. The upper face of the handle is enamelled with a blue background and red pattern.

The letters are moulded in relief below the rim. Letter height 5mm. There are serifs on the letters and the As are unbarred. The text comprised 43 letters of which two are incomplete and two are missing. The original drawing by Vaselle, prepared in 1949 and published by Heurgon in *JRS* 41 (1951) 23, shows the bottom of L and only one leg of A, with a complete S on the other side of the break (Figure 4.3 in this volume was prepared later to indicate the position of the coloured enamelling and does not show the L and the A and only the bottom half of the S). Only a regularly spaced N and an I would fill the gap:

MAIS ABALLAVA VXELODVNVM CAMBOGLA[NI]S BANNA ESICA

By comparison with the Rudge Cup the starting point for the text should be the same: Bowness-on-Solway, Burgh-by-Sands, Stanwix, Castlesteads, Birdoswald and Great Chesters. The names are in different coloured enamelled panels alternating green and blue.

Ilam Pan (*AE* 2004, 857; Tomlin and Hassall 2004, 344-345, no. 24)

Found in 2003 in the parish of Ilam in Staffordshire. Ownership shared between the British Museum, Tullie House Museum and Gallery, Carlisle and the Potteries Museum and Art Gallery, Stoke-on-Trent.

Figure 1.3. The Ilam Pan

A copper-alloy pan. Diameter on line of inscription 94mm; diameter at rim about 90mm; diameter at the foot ring about 54mm; height 47mm. Scroll. Decorated with eight evenly-spaced, incised roundels in red, blue, green, and possibly yellow enamel.

The letters are incised and filled with turquoise inlay. Letter height 3.5-4mm. There is an incised setting out line. The As are unbarred. The text comprises 56 letters:

RIGORE VALI AELI DRACONIS MAIS COGGABATA
VXELODVNVM CAMMOGIANNA

Since there is no punctuation on the inscription, the start point is significant. The inscription could read:

Bowness-on-Solway, Drumburgh, Stanwix, Castlesteads along the line of the Wall, [owned or made by] Aelius Draco;
Bowness-on-Solway, Drumburgh, Stanwix, Castlesteads along the line of Hadrian's Wall, [owned or made by] Draco;
along the line of the Wall, Aelius Draco [owned or made this], Bowness-on-Solway, Drumburgh, Stanwix, Castlesteads;
[owned or made by] Draco, Bowness-on-Solway, Drumburgh, Stanwix, Castlesteads along the line of Hadrian's Wall.

Tomlin and Hassall acknowledged that by comparison with the Rudge Cup and Amiens Patera, as well as logically, the start should be MAIS. However, they argued that the start lay with RIGORE, on the basis that 'there is a space before MAIS, whereas CAMMOGIANNA crowds against RIGORE, which suggests that DRACONIS was already there when MAIS was cut, but that RIGORE preceded CAMMOGIANNA. CAMMOG is quite generously drawn, whereas IANNA is noticeably smaller in height, as if to save space before RIGORE, which it almost touches. There is apparently no separation between RIGORE and VALI, except that VALI is lower in height, something which was forced on the engraver by the encroaching band of decoration below; nor did he leave a gap before AELI, or between it and DRACONIS; after that there is the space already mentioned before MAIS, and minimal separation of the place-names which follow, at its slightest between VXELODVNVM and CAMMOGIANNA. The generous spacing given to L in VXELODVNVM, which resembles a separation, is due only to miscalculation.' (Tomlin and Hassall 2004, 344, n. 45). Jackson in this volume has suggested that DRACONIS appears to have been given greatest prominence both in terms of letter size and spacing and that this may have been the first word.

Hildburgh Fragment (Cowen and Richmond 1935, 322-324)

Found between Zamora and León in northern Spain. Acquired by the Victoria and Albert Museum in 1949, London.

Fragment of a bronze vessel, possibly a flask. Restored diameter about 170mm; surviving height 80mm. Decorated in a similar geometric pattern to

Figure 1.4. The Hildburgh Fragment

the Rudge Cup and Amiens Patera. At the bottom are narrow triangles facing down, with a scroll above. There are then three rows of small rectangles. Above this there is an alternating pattern. One consists of a square containing four small squares and two crescents, on the lines of the Rudge Cup, but with the upper 'crenellations' sloping in the style of the Bath Pan. In between is a pattern of four leaves of turquoise enamel. The border between the upper motifs is red enamel; the scroll and the background to the leaves are blue enamel; the triangles at the bottom, the rows of three squares, the upper squares and crescents and the centre of the leaves are in turquoise enamel.

There are traces of incisions below the broken edge which could be the remains of letters but no sense can be made of them.

Beadlam Pan (*RIB* II. 2, 2415.54; *Britannia* 4 (1973) 334, n. 38)

Found in 1969 at Beadlam villa, Helmsley, North Yorkshire. Now with English Heritage.

Part of the rim and wall of a bronze pan. Restored diameter 173mm; surviving height 40mm. Decoration: a meander pattern, possibly represented foliage, outlined in pale blue enamel.

The letters are moulded in relief below the rim. They are followed by a zig-zag pattern. There are serifs on the letters. The surviving text has five letters:

]ICITR

This can perhaps be restored as [fel]ICIT(e)R (*RIB*) or [HISP(ANIAE)] CIT(E)R(IORIS) (*Britannia* 4 (1973) 334).

Bath Pan (*RIB* II. 2, 2415.60; Cunliffe 1988, 14, no. 23; 55, no. 23).

Found in 1979 in the Sacred Spring in the Roman baths at Bath. Now in Roman Baths Museum, Bath.

Figure 1.5. The Bath Pan

A bronze pan. Diameter at rim 94mm; height 45mm; length of handle 42mm. Decoration: moulded geometric pattern in the style of the Rudge Cup. A row of diagonally cut incisions run along the bottom and across the top, but in the opposite direction. The main decoration consists of alternating patterns, one consisting of four small squares surmounted by two crescents and the other triangles divided by breaks and with crescents below. At the top and bottom of the squares, the dividing line has three 'crenellations' in the form of the Hildburgh Fragment rather than the Rudge Cup and Amiens Patera.

The handle bears a votive inscription in punched dots: DIISVM[...] | CODON[... which may be read as: DE(AE) SV(LI) M[IN(ERVAE)] ...

Table 1.1. A comparison of the decorative motifs on several of the vessels (prepared by Lindsay Allason-Jones). * indicates the presence of the motif; X indicates that it is not present

Vessel	D1	D2	D3	D4	D5	D6	D7	D8	D9	D10	D11
Hildburgh	*	*	*	*	*	*	X	*	X	X	X
Rudge	X	*	X	*	X	X	*	*	*	X	X
Bath	X	X	*	*	*	*	X	upside down	X	*	X
Amiens	X	*	*	*	X	X	*	*	*	X	X
Harwood	*	X	X	X	*	X	X	X	X	X	X
Braughing	*	X	X	X	*	X	X	X	X	*	X
Linlithgow	*	X	X	X	*	X	X	X	X	*	X
Ilam	X	X	X	X	X	X	X	X	*	X	*

Decoration 1 Triangles
Decoration 2 Rows of rectangles
Decoration 3 Petalled motifs
Decoration 4 Running line
Decoration 5 Scrolls
Decoration 6 Peltae down

Decoration 7 Opposed peltae
Decoration 8 'Turrets'
Decoration 9 Inscription
Decoration 10 Short oblique lines
Decoration 11 Other

Chapter 2

Enamelled Vessels of Roman Britain

Ernst Künzl

INTRODUCTION

The Romans invented a line of business still alive today: travellers' souvenirs (Künzl and Koeppel 2002; Künzl 2008). At famous places like Athens, Ephesos or Alexandria Roman tourists could buy the same souvenirs we still do: small-scale copies of famous statues, glasses decorated with waterfront pictures of tourist sites, miniature portraits of celebrities and more of this kind.

THE ART OF ENAMELLING IN GREECE

The art of enamelling can be traced back at least to the second millennium BC when we know of enamelled finger-rings from a grave of the twelfth century BC in Western Cyprus (The Seventh British Museum Enamel Colloquium, 83: Tomb 8 at Kouklia Evrete, Western Cyprus). Enamel was a widespread decoration: excavators found enamel inlays in the golden jewellery of a princess at Kurgan Aržan 2 (Tuva region, Siberia), a tomb of the seventh century BC (Armbruster 2007). As with nearly everything in ancient culture, this technique was developed in Greece, where we find delicate gold jewellery in combination with enamelled parts. A spectacular gold necklace ('pectorale') was found in the tumulus of a Scythian king of the age of Alexander the Great, the Tolstaja Mogila in Southern Ukraine (Mozolevskij 1979; L'or des Scythes 1991, 72-79). On this wonderful example of the art of a Greek goldsmith we see many traces of enamel, especially on the flowers (green and other colours). A fine gold medallion – part of a hair-net – from early Hellenistic Macedonia shows the goddess Nike (Victory) with enamelled wings (now mostly corroded), surrounded by a ring of garnets and green glass stones imitating emeralds (Künzl 2000). Greek gold jewellery was always very colourful.

CELTIC CORALS AND ENAMELS

Ancient public opinion regarded Britain as an island of metal which could provide gold, silver and other metals (Frere 1987, 275). Philostratus of Lemnos in the third century specifically referred to enamelled metalwork, reporting that it was a typical product of the people near Oceanus (*tous en*

Okeáno barbárous) – that is, the north-west coasts of the empire, including the British Isles (Philostratus, *Imagines* I, 28, 3).

The Celts began to decorate metal by using other materials. Their favourite was at first red coral, traditionally worn as an amulet (Pliny the Elder, *Natural History* 37, 164). Ancient writers mention red coral as medicine (Pliny the Elder, *Natural History* 32, 24; Celsus, *de medicina* 5, 6 ff.). Ovid explains that the corals were drops of blood from Medusa's neck that had fallen into the sea and petrified into their present shape (*Metamorphoses* 4, 744-752). The Celts used corals from the beginning of the La Tène period (450 BC), but later they substituted red enamel, as on the famous Battersea and Witham shield bosses (Stead 1985, 13 fig. 12; 56 fig. 77 and front cover; Stead 1985, 54 and title page; Freestone *et al.* 2003) (Figure 2.1).

Figure 2.1. The medallion of the Battersea Shield. Diameter 290mm. Bronze and red enamel. Celtic, dating to about 100 BC

ROMAN BRITAIN'S CELTIC BACKGROUND

'Roman' in Britain does not mean the same as 'Roman' in Gaul or in Spain as Britain never became 'Romanised' to the same degree; or, to express it the other way round, we find more surviving Celtic elements in Britain than we do on the Continent. When the Romans crossed the Channel under the Emperor Claudius in 43 the empire's Romanising energy had already considerably diminished. The Romanisation of Britain was in many ways nothing but a surface veneer. Boudicca's Revolt in the year 60 during the reign of the Emperor Nero almost ended Roman rule in Britain before Romanisation had really begun. As it was, Boudicca lost her last battle, and the Romans probably attempted to liquidate the Celtic intellectual class of druids and destroy their sanctuaries. But Celtic tradition survived in Roman disguise and one of the most impressive examples is the Romano-British production of enamelled vessels, unique within the empire (Roman enamels in general: Henry 1933; Moore 1978; Künzl 1995; Künzl 2008).

Among decorated brooches we encounter types peculiar to Roman Britain. Dragonesque brooches of the decades around 100 show clearly the survival of the Late La Tène Celtic taste, which liked to combine animals, plants and inorganic elements in sophisticated compositions (Bulmer 1938; Feachem 1951; Feachem 1968; Johns 1996, 151-

Figure 2.2. A dragonesque fibula. Height 62mm. Bronze and enamel

153; 183-184). The Dragonesque brooches are an entirely British affair (Figure 2.2).

FLASK MOULDS FROM CASTLEFORD

Archaeologists agree that most of the larger enamelled vessels of the Roman period came from Britain. The distribution map of these enamelled objects focuses on Britain, but also includes France, the Benelux countries, Germany, and elsewhere, including even Spain, Italy, and the Black Sea (Künzl 1995, 44-45, fig. 6). How could we prove that a flask like the Pinguente find from Istria was produced in Britain and not in Italy? (De Linas 1884; Henry 1933, 145, pl. 1; Alföldi 1939, 357-358, pl. 31; Moore 1978, 327). There are arguments

Figure 2.3. The flask from Pinguente, Istria. Height 175mm. Bronze and enamel (red, blue, and green). Date: second century

based on style, but recent finds of vessel moulds from Castleford in Yorkshire (Figure 2.4) have now proved that such flasks were being produced in Britain in the years around 100 (Bayley 1995).

Castleford was a Roman fort and had both military and civilian settlements. In rubbish pits excavators found over 1,000 mould fragments for making flasks with enamelled decoration (Bayley 1995; Bayley and Budd 1998). The technique used was champlevé enamelling, the most common technique in Roman Britain for larger vessels: the artist would cast shallow pits of different shapes in the relatively thick wall of the vessel, fill them with coloured glass powder, and then heat the vessel to finish the enamelled design.

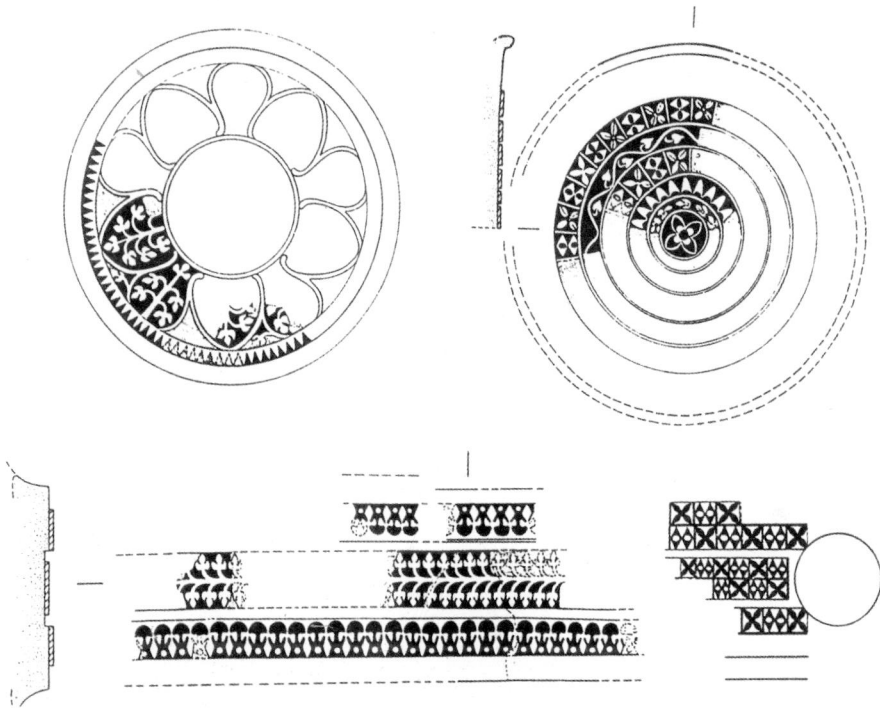

Figure 2.4. Flask moulds from Castleford, Yorkshire. Date: first to second century (Bayley 1995, fig. 6).

After the Castleford discoveries, we can take it for granted that some of the most distant finds – like decorated strigils (oil-scrapers) and alabastrons (unguent containers) from Gorgippia on the Black Sea, an alabastron from a shipwreck off Camarina in Sicily, and of course the Pinquente flask – are all of Romano-British origin (Leskow, et al., 1989, nos. 268 and 269; Di Stefano 1995; Di Vita et al. 1995).

TYPES OF ENAMELLED PRODUCTS FROM ROMAN BRITAIN

We can identify metalworkers in Roman Britain who came from the Continent and produced metal artefacts in a 'Roman' style – which means more or less a

Figure 2.5. The alabastron from Bartlow Hills, Ashdon, Essex (Barrow IV). Height 80mm. Bronze and enamel (red, blue, and green). Date: second century

Hellenistic style. On the other hand we also find in Britain artists working in a strong late La Tène tradition, and still trained in the lore of Celtic Britain's metalworking craft. Those dragonesque brooches are a supreme example.

Figure 2.6. The skillet from a sanctuary at Bad Pyrmont, Germany. Length 205mm; height 64mm. Bronze and enamel (blue and green). Date: second century

The market for enamelled vessels boomed from the late first century throughout the second. In the generation after Boudicca, bronze workers offered cups, skillets and toilet vessels like the one from Bartlow Hills (Figure 2.5) decorated with scrolls in Mediterranean style (Gage 1836, pl. 35; Henry 1933, 112, fig. 26, 2; Moore 1978, 326). Another design featured a pentagon combined with floral motifs; a prominent find is the skillet from a Germanic open-air sanctuary at Bad Pyrmont, Germany (Moore 1978, 326; Teegen 1999, 220; 245-249, 364, pl. 17) (Figure 2.6).

Bronze cockerels that were offered to Mercury and other gods were also enamelled, with examples extending from London, across the Channel, down the Maas valley, and as far as Cologne in the

Figure 2.7. The cockerel from Cologne, Germany. Height 130mm. Bronze and enamel (blue, red, green, and yellow). Date: second century

Rhine valley (Figure 2.7), that is, along one of the area's most important trade routes (Henry 1933, 141, fig. 43, 1; Menzel 1986, 59-60 nos. 122, pl. 78; Künzl 2008, 25).

There were also hexagonal boxes with millefiori enamel decoration ('thousand-flower', where rods of coloured glass are fused together), found from Britain to the Black Sea; and in this case they are known to have been produced on the Continent as well as in Britain (Elsenham) (Henry 1933, 135, fig. 41, 3; 42, 1-4; Potter and Johns 1992, 134, pl. 8; Johns 1993). These charming little boxes served as ink-pots or as containers for cosmetics (Figure 2.8).

Figure 2.8. The hexagonal box from Elsenham, Essex. Height 46mm. Bronze and 'millefiori' enamel. Date: second century

THE CELTIC UNDERCURRENT

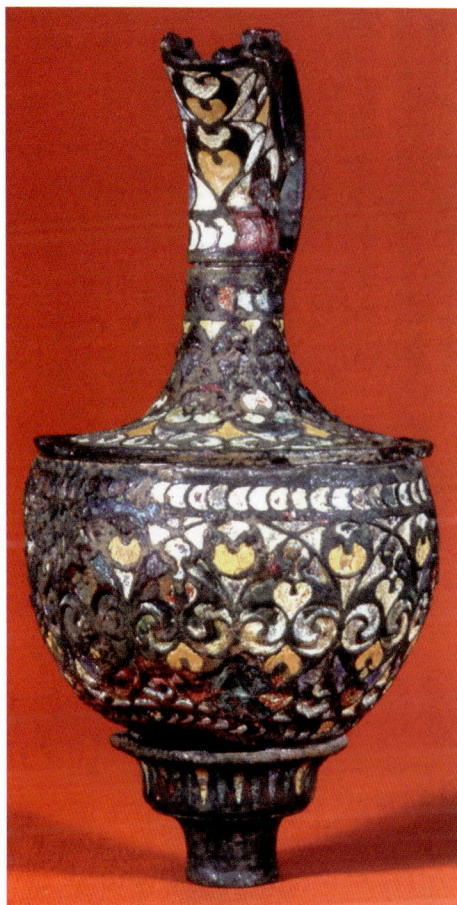

Figure 2.9. A jug from a grave in northern France. Height 247mm. Bronze and enamel (red, blue, green, and yellow). Date: about 100

Figure 2.10. A *patera* from a grave in northern France. Length 365mm. Bronze and enamel (red, blue, and green). Date: about 100

Figure 2.11. Electronic reconstruction of the design of the jug, fig. 2.9

Dragonesque brooches were not the only example of Celtic tradition in the Roman Empire: there was a strong Celtic element in the decoration of some extraordinary enamelled vessels found in Britain, France, and even Spain. All show non-figural decoration in La Tène style, in which Celtic ornament has been created geometrically using compasses (Stead and Hughes 1997).

Very splendid examples are the jug and *patera* from northern France on display in Mainz (Künzl 1995, 40-43, fig. 2-5; Künzl 2008, 27) (Figures 2.9 and 2.10). They were used as a hand-washing set: a servant poured water from the jug over his master's hands and collected it in the *patera*. While the *patera* is decorated in a more Mediterranean style, the jug represents Britain's best 'neo-Celtic' style from the years around 100 (Figure 2.11).

On the Continent, after 160, there was a cultural fashion sometimes called 'the Celtic renaissance'. Roman Britain had no need of one as Celtic style, Celtic ornaments, Celtic taste had never totally disappeared. Romano-British enamelled products are testimony to that. In the imaginary sales catalogues of Romano-British craftsmen in the second century, enamelled vessels would no doubt have figured prominently.

HADRIAN'S WALL SOUVENIRS

A spectacular variety of the Roman souvenir industry seems to have developed on Hadrian's Wall in the second century. Soldiers could buy *paterae* (pans or skillets) decorated in colourful enamel that depicted aspects of the Wall. Some, like the so-called Rudge Cup and the Amiens Patera, combined an image of the Wall with a list of military place-names, all of them along the western half of the Wall between Bowness and Great Chesters (Frontispiece, Figures 1.1, 1.2, 2.12). A second group of these souvenirs (finds from Bath and northern Spain) shows only the simplified image of the Wall, without any inscriptions, suggesting perhaps that these products were sold right along the northern frontier (Figures 1.4, 1.5). A third design is known since the discovery in 2003 of the Ilam Pan, where the artist has given a list of forts but replaced the Wall with a flamboyant motif of scrolls – creating one of the most beautiful pieces of Romano-British enamel art to have come down to us. Vessels of this shape formed parts of Roman drinking-sets, especially for mulled wine, perhaps contributing to the ambience when veterans got together to chat about old times 'in the service'.

THE ILAM PAN: A SPECIAL CASE

The Amiens Patera lists six places, the Rudge Cup five, so with a list only of four places and with its second part of the inscription (*rigore vali Aeli Draconis*) the Ilam Pan is a special case (Figure 1.3). *Rigore vali* seems to refer to the Wall; it could mean that the four named places were situated on the Wall line. We can take for granted, furthermore, that Aelius Draco is a

Figure 2.12. The Rudge Cup. (After Bruce 1880, pl. after p. 138)

Figure 2.13. The Hildburgh Fragment. Electronic reconstruction.

personal name, and so the text should be an abbreviation: *[ex officina] Aeli Draconis* (from the workshop of Aelius Draco).

The Ilam Pan inscription is engraved and not cast. That means the product in the beginning had nothing to do with the Wall souvenirs; it was an all-purpose vessel. The inscription was added afterwards and changed the vessel into a Wall souvenir. So the Ilam Pan plays a very important role. Until now we could not be sure that the vessels of the Rudge Cup type were a success with the Roman market or not. That *we* appreciate these vessels is no argument at all: it is a wide-spread mistake among historians and archaeologists to assume that the Romans liked the same things we do. Four vessels (Rudge, Amiens, Bath, Hildburgh) are such a tiny group that it is impossible to speak of statistics or of markets. But now the Ilam Pan has changed the picture by the simple fact that the customer paid some craftsman to add four place-names at the western end of Hadrian's Wall to the vessel. This seems to prove that these Wall souvenirs were a success, worth being imitated.

The vessels without inscriptions could be sold along the Wall between Bowness-on-Solway and Wallsend. We also have to take into account that they were made for illiterate people. Illiteracy is still a problem in modern European states, where we can calculate a illiteracy rate of about five per cent according to statistics: four million individuals in Germany 2009 are provably illiterate (= five per cent); comparable numbers exist for Switzerland; for Eastern European countries we have to guess. In Roman times education was reserved for the upper classes and the rich. The aristocrats of the Roman Empire accounted for less than one per cent of the population in the first century (theoretically assumed to be 50-80 millions). It is nearly impossible to determine numbers, but we have to consider that people who could read and write formed a relatively small minority within the Roman Empire - despite all the inscriptions, libraries, military diplomas, Vindolanda writing tablets, and so on (Duncan-Jones 1977; Harris 1989. Cf. also Kunow 1983; Blanck 1992, 22 ff. and Donderer 1995. Alföldi 1999, 23-27 is far too optimistic).

THE DATE OF THE SOUVENIRS

We can assume that these vessels were produced when the Wall was fully functional. This includes only a few years in the 130s, but it seems unlikely that the production of these souvenirs had already started before Hadrian's death in 138.

Under the Emperor Antoninus Pius, who moved the army 160km (100 miles) north to the Antonine Wall, there was no real reason to produce souvenirs of this kind. But with the year 161 or so the whole situation had changed. The new emperor Marcus Aurelius ended the Antonine Wall episode and returned to the line of Hadrian's Wall. In the western part of the Wall, the area of Hadrian's Turf Wall, many places were now rebuilt in stone, and the

Figure 2.14. Hadrian's Wall. Artist's impression by Michael J. Moore

Figure 2.15. Palisade Upper German *limes* at Zugmantel, north of Wiesbaden, Germany. Date: second century. (*photograph: author*)

area would have gained a lot of new respectability. This was the right moment to create these souvenirs.

So I suggest we see in our enamelled souvenirs works of the late Antonine age (161-192). These are general observations, because the iconography does not help at all. The design is what we would call in our electronic world an icon or a pictogram: it means 'military architecture', and combined with the place-names it certainly means the Wall, but, in relationship to the question of ramparts and crenellations for the frontier, our vessels do not contribute anything useful.

The craftsman of the Bath Pan (Figure 1.5) misunderstood the design: he placed the rectangular pattern in the space between the turrets. Without the help of the Rudge Cup and the Amiens Patera nobody could recognize in the Bath vessel design a picture of Hadrian's Wall.

Why place the Wall motif on souvenirs, which was unique in the context of all the Roman souvenir production? Perhaps because Hadrian's Wall was an impressive military architectural structure (Figure 2.14), contrasted with the boring ramparts and palisades of Upper Germany (Figure 2.15) or the open lines along the North African desert. Basically also, Hadrian's Wall was a frontier line to control movements and traffic, as were the other boundaries of the Roman Empire. The Wall was not a place to be defended like a medieval castle: 'the Roman army was primarily intended to fight in the open and would if possible move out to engage the enemy long before the Wall was reached' (Breeze and Dobson 2000, 42). But Hadrian's Wall looked better than the frontier lines elsewhere – and this was the decisive point. Hadrian's Wall was something special, a place to remember.

Chapter 3

The Rudge Cup

Lindsay Allason-Jones

This paper offers a detailed description of the Rudge Cup, an explanation as to why it is so called, and a short discourse on how it got to Alnwick Castle, where it currently resides.

The vessel itself is small, only 46mm high with a rim diameter of 89-93mm – it is slightly squashed but was originally circular. It has a basal diameter of 58mm. It has bulging walls, a beaded rim and a beaded base rim. Its champlevé enamelling can be divided into three zones. The lower has a grid of rectangles resembling coursed masonry, outlined in reserved metal, with nicks along the upper and lower edges. The rectangles have contained enamel, the surviving traces of which are green; so the original enamel may have been green but more probably white. The central range, which emerges from the lower register, has pairs of alternating rectangles, 14 in all, one type

Figure 3.1. The Rudge Cup, a. BANNA.A.MAIS; b. ABALLAVAVXELOD[;
c. CAMBOGLANSBAN[

being subdivided into four rectangles with crenellations along the top, the second has nicked edges containing two pairs of back-to-back peltate motifs, each with a reserved dot. Traces of red and green – or again, more probably white enamel – survive (Figure 3.2). The upper field is a plain grooved channel with letters in reserved metal, about which more later. No trace of enamel survives in this field, the edges of which, like the lower register, have little oblique nicks.

Figure 3.2. The Rudge Cup showing traces of enamel. (*photograph: author*)

It is possible that more enamel survived when the Cup was first found. An illustration in John Collingwood Bruce's *Catalogue of Antiquities at Alnwick Castle* shows a red enamelled line delineating the Wall line, with blue and green enamel alternating elsewhere (Bruce 1880, no. 746, 139-140) (Figure 2.12). Again, there is no hint of the colour of the enamel in the channel around the letters.

There is no trace of a handle, although there are rough areas on the inner surface above a hole in the side (Figure 3.3). This hole, however, does not look like the result of a handle being wrenched away but is more probably the result of the vessel hitting a hard object when thrown into the well where it was discovered or a pick hitting it during excavation. If there was a handle, it must have been of the type that simply clips into position, but the rim shows no evidence for its existence.

John Horsley, whom Lord Hertford 'favoured … with a sight of the vessel' soon after it was discovered, commented that 'the bottom of this vessel is broken off from it, but is yet also in his lordship's possession' (Horsley 1732, 329). There is no further mention of a base in the subsequent descriptions

Figure 3.3. The Rudge Cup showing damage from the outside. (*photograph: author*)

and the base had completely disappeared by the time the Rudge Cup reached Alnwick Castle (Bruce 1880, 139). Horsley went on to mention that the base was thinner than the rest of the vessel, which, with the clean finish of the vessel walls, suggests that it was made as a separate piece and soldered into position, although evidence of soldering is presumed rather than particularly obvious. The surface of the base ring shows clear file marks, which would provide a key for the soldering (Figure 3.5).

There are traces of a deposit on the inner surface, which initially looks like rust but closer examination throws doubt on this. No analysis has been done on this deposit. Sadly, as the Cup has experienced various conservation techniques over the years, it is probably too late for analysis.

When John Cowen described the decoration in his joint paper with Ian Richmond in 1935, he had clearly made up his mind as to what it represented: 'a fortification consisting of a wall strengthened at regular

Figure 3.4. The Rudge Cup showing damage from the inside. (*photograph: author*)

intervals by crenellated turrets. The presentation is purely conventional, and the schematic manner in which it is conceived is further emphasised by the treatment of the surface, which is entirely covered with rectangular panels of enamel calculated to give the impression, rather than a faithful rendering, of coursed masonry' (Cowen and Richmond 1935, 317). He goes on, however, to mention that 'the spaces between the turrets are filled by a purely decorative element consisting of pairs of crescents' (Cowen and Richmond 1935, 317-8). Cowen was of the opinion that his military interpretation was glaringly obvious and expressed his surprise that no-one had noticed it before.

Figure 3.5. The base of the Rudge Cup. (*photograph: author*)

Cowen stated that 'the nature of the turrets with their crenellated tops in bronze relief against the enamelled background is quite unmistakable' (Cowen and Richmond 1935, 318). From this statement until the present day, any argument as to whether the Wall was crenellated and the debate on the form of the turrets has used the Rudge Cup as supporting evidence. Cowen went on to claim that 'on the Rudge Cup we have the only contemporary representation of the Roman Wall known to have survived to our times'. Whether the pattern represents turrets, crenellated or not, is still the subject of debate; it is possible that they represent forts projecting from the Wall with the crossed line representing the roads through a four-gate fort. The 'crenellations' may represent crenellations on the fort walls or on the fort gateways. However, as no-one has ever suggested the alternating squares, with their peltate motifs, are anything other than decorative, it is not clear how relevant or important the 'crenellations' actually are.

The 36 evenly spaced letters are in reserved metal within a moulded channel:

.A.MAISABALLAVAVXELODVMCAMBOGLANSBANNA

They are arranged in a continuous strip with only two stop marks, before and after one of the As. The letters have serifs and the As do not have a cross bar. It should be emphasised that the Rudge Cup letters are in reserved metal, as are those on the Amiens Patera. The Ilam Pan letters, on the other hand, have been cut into the metal.

Considerable attention has been given over the years to what the letters on the Rudge Cup mean but it is now agreed that they give the names of five of the forts in the western sector of Hadrian's Wall: *Mais* (Bowness-on-Solway), *Aballava* (Burgh-by-Sands), *Uxelod(un)um* (Stanwix), *Camboglanna* (Castlesteads) and *Banna* (Birdoswald). The A at the beginning is read as the preposition of Mais (Rivet and Smith 1979, 232-4; Holder, this volume).

This interpretation was not arrived at without a struggle. In a somewhat confused paper in *Archaeologia Aeliana* for 1876, a local Northumbrian worthy, called Ralph Carr-Ellison, was very scathing about the suggestion that the letters named forts on Hadrian's Wall. In his opinion, 'the key-word Mais is not necessarily in the ablative; nay, much more naturally it falls into the dative' (Carr-Ellison 1876, 263). He decided that the names were people's names, with the text reporting the donation of the cup by a triad of men called Aballava, Uxelodum, and Camboglannis Banna. The word Mais, he expounded, came from 'Maii', 'a latinised British word signifying Men of the Plains'; his evidence was mined from the Welsh. The first letter 'A', which gave such trouble to his colleagues, he firmly stated to be an abbreviation of 'amicus' and he interpreted the whole inscription as 'To the friendly men of the plains, Abavalla, Uxelodum and Banna present this cup' – where Camboglannis fitted into this interpretation is left unexplained. He concluded that part of his discourse with the supposition that 'it might be inferred that these Friendly Neighbours had assisted them [the soldiers] in rearing the wall represented upon the object thus given'.

At this point Mr Carr-Ellison seems to have changed his mind. He plunged headfirst into the classical languages and offered an alternative suggestion, stating 'but since such an interpretation of Mais occurred to me last year, I have found so many instances of Graeco-Latin adaptation and phraseology in the epigraphy of The Wall, that I deem it necessary to examine every uncertain term with regard to a possibly Hellenistic origin' (Carr-Ellison 1876, 263).

Following this dangerous course he then found that *maia* in ancient Greek 'was the designation of the women who acted as attendants on the sick', particularly those who acted as midwives, but he managed to convince himself that it was a term 'perfectly applicable to whatsoever females were in attendance in such hospitalary apartments and quarters as a Roman army was able to provide for its many wounded, ailing and infirm, and who would be the best assistants to the medical officers, and not seldom their able substitutes'. It is important to remember at this point that Carr-Ellison was writing less than 20 years after the end of the Crimea War, during which Miss Florence Nightingale had changed people's attitudes to women nursing in military contexts. He continued by saying that 'we know that nearer to our own times, that is, in the middle ages, medicine and surgery were much in the hands of women, and were skilfully cultivated – even by ladies of high birth' (Carr-Ellison 1876, 263).

As a result of this delving into the Greek language and female emancipation, he concluded that 'owing to some unusually hard fighting and a consequent accumulation of wounded soldiers, or owing to some epidemic disease, the camps at Aballava, Uxelodunum and Camboglannis Banna had felt more than ordinary obligation and gratitude to the *curatrices* or nurses of their sick-quarters, and that in recognition of the signal services they conferred a number of sacrificial cups for libations'. So in two pages he has moved rapidly from saying that there was nothing in favour of saying that the names were of forts to saying that some of them are and translating the text to read:

> To the Kind Nurses – this cup we give –
> Aballava, Uxellodunum, Camboglannese Banna

Mr Carr-Ellison then continued a bad habit he had developed in the long Northumbrian winter nights, of transcribing Latin inscriptions into rhyming verse and offered the following as a reasonable translation of the Rudge Cup:

> To the Kind Nurses, Three Camps jointly gave
> The Mural Crown, for toils the sick to save.

Archaeologia Aeliana in the nineteenth century was the main medium through which the classicists and Wall scholars of the day debated the inscriptions which were appearing regularly in the area. Some of these debates got quite heated, with claims and counter claims being published each year. It is worth noting that Mr Carr-Ellison's contribution to the puzzle of the Rudge Cup, although published, was not commented upon in print.

Once the decision was made that the text referred to the names of forts in the Military Zone, there was still much debate as to which forts were intended. Mr Carr-Ellison, in his discourse was unclear where *Maia* was, whilst he thought that *Aballava* was 'situate where Papcastle now stands' (Carr-Ellison 1876, 263-4). In *The Place Names of Roman Britain,* Rivet and Smith argue that *Maia* is Bowness-on-Solway, *Aballava* is Burgh-by-Sands, *Uxelodunum* is Stanwix, *Camboglanna* is Castlesteads and *Banna* is Birdoswald (Rivet and Smith 1979, 232-3). The reasoning behind this and the derivations of the names are covered elsewhere in this volume; for the moment attention is simply drawn to the fact that all the vessels found so far refer to the forts in the western sector of the Wall.

It should be recalled that the accessibility of Hadrian's Wall is quite a recent phenomenon. It was only in 1848 that John Collingwood Bruce travelled along Hadrian's Wall with two of the Richardson family of artists and his son Gainsford, having been thwarted in his original intention of holidaying in

Rome by the political situation (Birley 1961, 26). On his return to Newcastle, Bruce gave a talk to the Literary and Philosophical Society of Newcastle upon Tyne, using the Richardson brothers' watercolours as visual aids. The members of the Literary and Philosophical Society expressed doubts as to the accuracy of the drawings, being particularly unconvinced that the forts survived as well as seemed to be indicated. This was because, with a few notable exceptions, few people ever went near the central sector of the Wall due to the activities of the Busy Gap Rogues, a band of outlaws who preyed on travellers in the area. Camden, for example, did not venture into the area because of what he referred to as 'the rank robbers thereabouts' (Camden 1600, 718). Most people's knowledge of the Wall, therefore, was based on the observations of John Horsley, William Stukeley and Roger Gale but Stukeley and Gale's visit to the Wall was in 1725, the same year that the Rudge Cup was discovered, and the tale of their journey was not published until 1776 (Stukeley 1776). The earliest comments on the Rudge Cup, therefore, were offered in a climate of limited knowledge and considering the limitations of that knowledge some of those comments were very impressive.

In his *Britannia Romana*, John Horsley considered that the west end of the Wall was the part of the frontier that was in the most danger, 'and consequently, [he said] it became more necessary for the several garrisons to enter into a stricter confederacy for their mutual strength and support' (Horsley 1732, 330). Clearly he had doubts about the neighbourliness of the Novantae and the inhabitants of Ireland.

Sir Richard Colt Hoare, who published a note on the Rudge Cup in 1812, was wary about entering the lists regarding the use of the object, contenting himself with the statement that 'The learned Gale conjectures it to have been a *patera* used in libations by the people of those towns that are mentioned upon it' (Colt Hoare 1812, 121-3). The 'learned Gale', of course, was particularly interested as it was likely he had just visited some of the sites mentioned on the Cup. Colt Hoare went on to explain to his readers that 'sacrifices were generally offered by the ancients, when they met together upon any solemn occasion; sometimes even when they were assembled only for mirth and feasting; why then might there not have been an alliance or society formed among those five neighbouring places and perhaps a feast annually, or more frequently observed by them, when they jointly made their libations out of one common *patera* inscribed with all their names, as a token of their friendship and unanimity?' (Colt Hoare 1812).

As can be deduced from the foregoing, the names mentioned on the Cup lead invariably to the question of what was it for. Cowen was not keen on the Cup being used for pouring libations but considered that, while its shape made it perfectly serviceable to drink out of, he felt that 'its small size counts against such a purpose, unless, indeed we imagine the contents it was designed to hold have been of the highest rarity, or of the most formidable potence' (Cowen and Richmond 1935, 311). He preferred to see it as a container for sweetmeats or as a cruet for salt or vinegar. Its diameter of 89-93mm and height of 46mm makes it about the size of a breakfast teacup and capable of containing more liquid than a Dragendorff 27 vessel. It is unlikely John Cowen served helpings of any liquid, other than beer, to his guests in larger amounts.

Heurgon's view, set out in his paper on the Amiens Patera in 1951, was that 'no doubt they were made for the Army on the Wall, and the soldiers were pleased to take them back in their baggage when they went home' (Heurgon 1951, 24). He implied that the vessels were produced and bought as souvenirs, rather like objects bought as presents from a seaside resort. His presumption was that a soldier would buy a vessel which included the name of the fort in which he had served. This idea he based on the discovery of the Hildburgh Fragment in north-west Spain, between León and Zamora. He offered the suggestion that the Fragment had belonged to an officer of the First Cohort of Asturians who had returned home after serving on the Wall. Unfortunately, for this argument there is no lettering on the Hildburgh Fragment so we cannot link any of the forts on the Wall occupied by Asturians with this vessel. Cowen, on the other hand, saw the Rudge Cup as part of a set, the others presumably giving the names of the forts in the central and eastern sectors (Cowen and Richmond 1935, 311). In support of his argument he drew his readers' attention to other examples of metal vessels with place-names on them, such as the four silver vessels found at Aqua Apollinaris in 1852 which seem to provide between them the names of places on the route from Cadiz to Rome (Holder, this volume).

Cowen and Richmond believed that the Rudge Cup, the Amiens Patera and the Hildburgh Fragment formed parts of sets. This suggests that there should be two others in each set, one covering the central sector, and the other dealing with the eastern forts (Cowen and Richmond 1935, 312). That we now have three similar vessels, all of which cover the western sector, may suggest that there never was such a set. The fact that the Amiens Patera included *Aesica*/Great Chesters indicates that there was some variation in what could be bought, whilst the manner of the Ilam Pan's lettering implies that one could buy a custom made vessel with one's name on it – presumably for a higher cost.

The question of what they were intended to be used for is, probably, unanswerable. No doubt the purchasers had their own plans for them – whether to give them away as presents, use them to pour libations (as suggested by Colt Hoare) or just to place on the Roman equivalent of a mantlepiece to remind them of their military service on the Wall. The evidence simply does not survive for a firm conclusion to be reached and it may be that there is no single answer.

The next question is: where was the Rudge Cup made and when? Françoise

Henry, in her review of western enamelling in the Roman period in 1930, was of the opinion that the Rudge Cup was made in Britain (Henry 1933, 112). This opinion was based largely on the inscription including, as it does, British place-names. She was diffident about this conclusion, however, probably being aware that many souvenirs bought around the world are actually made somewhere else – in the nineteenth century, for example, a whole industry of making international souvenirs developed in Birmingham. Her suggestion was supported by John Cowen, who compared the Cup to the cups from Braughing and Maltbœk, a *patera* from West Lothian and the handled vessel from Bartlow Hills (Cowen and Richmond 1935, 320) (Figure 2.5, 5.8 and 9.1). He was of the opinion that all these vessels came from a single workshop, basing his theory on the similarity between the decorative motifs of olive wreath, ivy scroll and what he called 'backgammon dentellation'. Sadly, he had to admit that none of these motifs appear on the Rudge Cup (see Table 1.1). He considered all the vessels to be from the first half of the second century, though he may have been influenced by his knowledge of the date of the building of Hadrian's Wall rather than stylistic considerations.

Cowen also discussed an enamelled vessel from Harwood in Northumberland (which is in the British Museum and is very much shorter and wider and has no decorative similarities to the Rudge Cup, other than the fact that it is enamelled) and a bowl from Bingen on the Rhine. The former he presumed to be a later copy of the Braughing type. The latter he dismissed as being irrelevant to any discussion on dating. Whilst it is true that the Bingen bowl has no names on it, it is very much of the same form as the Rudge Cup, with a similar outline, rim and foot; the difference lies in its decoration of an all-over enamelled square design, similar to the coursed masonry on the Rudge Cup. He also considered a group of vessels which he ascribed to a Belgian school and which Françoise Henry thought was contemporary with the British examples, but Cowen again rejected them as having no contribution to make regarding the date or place of manufacture of the Rudge Cup.

He was firmly of the opinion that the Cup was made by a school of enamelling based in the south-east of England and doubted that the Cup was ever on the Wall itself, suggesting that the buyer may have bought it in the South as a reminder of his time in the North. Cowen did, however, agree with Henry that the Hildburgh Fragment was made by the same hand as that of the Rudge Cup. He actually borrowed the Fragment from Dr W. L. Hildburgh and made some useful comments about it in his paper on the Rudge Cup – he appears to have been the only person at the time to see the Fragment and certainly the only one to notice some incised lines in the space where the inscriptions are on the other vessels. These incisions, however, are inscribed into the metal – as on the Ilam Pan – and what little survives seems to suggest possible post-Roman lettering.

Cowen also suggested that a belt hanger from South Shields, with *Utere*

Felix enamelled on it, was also made by the same hand. His argument was that the shape of the lettering was the same as on the Rudge Cup whilst there were also back-to-back crescents (Cowen and Richmond 1935, 325). Since his observations, however, several of the *Utere Felix* hangers have been found and it is likely that their similarity to the Rudge Cup is purely coincidental (cf. Holder, this volume).

In regard to the date of the Cup: it might be presumed that it cannot be earlier than about 125 as most of the forts were not completed before then. Sadly, none of the vessels include names of forts as far east as Carrawburgh, acknowledged as being the latest fort to be built and thus a very useful site for dating purposes. Cowen and his colleagues suggested a date, on stylistic grounds, of about 150 but David Breeze and Brian Dobson have pointed out that this was a period when the Wall was largely abandoned in favour of the Antonine Wall – not the optimum time to be mass-producing a souvenir (Breeze and Dobson 2000, 291). It is probable that the vessel was made fairly soon after the Wall was completed in the early 130s, when the frontier was still new and exciting, when the turrets were still in use and when the people who built it still had a sense of pride and ownership and when the garrison of the frontier is likely to have been at its peak.

The forts named, if we follow the modern translations, are all in Cumbria and arranged in order from west to east. The fort at Drumburgh, however, is missing. Sadly, there has been very little excavation at Drumburgh so it is difficult to say if it was built late in the sequence – the presumption is that it was not, so why is it missing? Breeze and Dobson have suggested that it was because of its small size – that is, it may not have been regarded at the time as being a proper Wall fort (Breeze and Dobson 2000, 292).

The Amiens Patera includes *Aesica* (Great Chesters) but misses out Carvoran. Breeze and Dobson argue that this is because Carvoran is set slightly to the south of the Wall, beyond the Vallum, so again may not have been regarded as a proper Wall fort. Richmond pointed out that Carvoran is also missing in the *Ravenna Cosmography* (Cowen and Richmond 1935, 334-341). Yet Castlesteads is included, although also offset from the Wall. This fort, however, is within the area delimited by the Vallum so perhaps that made it a 'proper Wall fort'. Breeze and Dobson reject the idea that the listing of the forts on these enamelled vessels is based on an Itinerary on the grounds that there was no Military Way linking the forts until a period much later than is likely for the Cup (Breeze and Dobson 2000, 240). This may not be strictly relevant – even with a link road, there was still the Stanegate, and travellers along the Stanegate should either have been heading for the Wall forts or using them for navigational purposes. The arguments for the inclusion, or not, of various forts seems to suggest the metalworker or metalworkers were aware of nuances of fort status, which might argue against the idea that the vessels were made at some distance from the Wall.

On the evidence currently available, it is not possible to say where the vessels were made. However, we can be sure that so far none has been found that came from the same mould as the Rudge Cup. The nearest to the Rudge Cup is the Amiens Patera – its body decoration of coursed masonry with the wider band of crenellated squares and pelta decorated squares is exactly the same, as is its method of using reserved metal to give the names of forts. The inclusion of Aesica in the lettering indicates a different mould, although it is likely that the Amiens Patera and the Rudge Cup were made by the same hand. The Hildburgh Fragment is bigger, and in some ways more elaborate, and does not appear to have included the names of forts, at least not in the same stiff lettering as the Rudge Cup and Amiens Patera. As was stated earlier, it is not likely that the same hand was responsible for the Rudge Cup and the Hildburgh Fragment although it is possible that they could have been made in the same workshop. The Ilam Pan is another matter altogether. Although the beaded rim is similar to the Rudge Cup and the Amiens Patera, the flared base is very different, as is the very florid, rather Celtic looking, enamelled decoration that takes up most of the body of the vessel. And then, of course, we have the completely different way of incising the lettering and the inclusion of a name, which may be that of an individual or the family name of the Emperor Hadrian, among the forts. It is doubtful that the Ilam Pan came from the same workshop as the other three vessels although obviously it is in the same genre.

WHY RUDGE?

The discovery of the cup is entangled in the history of the Percy family as well as the history of the Society of Antiquaries of London. It was in 1725 that a farmer discovered the remains of a building in an area called Rudge Coppice, which is near a village called Froxfield, 10.6km (6 miles) east of Marlborough in the county of Wiltshire. Colt Hoare suggested that the findspot was 'probably near the course of the Roman road which ran from the station of Cunetio, on the river Kennet, and that of Spinae at Speen Hill' (Hoare 1812, 121). By 'Cunetio' it is possible that he meant Mildenhall in Wiltshire; Spinae is less easy to identify but may mean the possible settlement at Woodspeen in Berkshire.

News of the discovery reached the Earl of Hertford who, at the time, was the president of the Society of Antiquaries of London – a position he held from 1724 to 1750. He decided that the find warranted a closer look and arranged for a proper excavation to be carried out. An account of the proceedings survives in a letter by the antiquary Lethieullier, which he wrote on 25 May 1726 to a Mr Wise, giving Lord Hertford's description of the excavations (Hoare 1812, 122). The main site was a building of Roman date; the discovery of a fine mosaic floor immediately placed it in the ranks of a villa – a description about which the modern Historic Environment Record for Wiltshire seems less certain. No work has been done on the site since Lord Hertford's activities and the only publication of the excavation is Colt Hoare's publication of the Lethieullier letter, so there is no confirmation that the site was a villa, although it seems probable.

The Cup was not found in the building itself but in a well close by. The well, it is recorded, was full of rubbish including several bones of what John Collingwood Bruce, in his *Catalogue of Antiquities at Alnwick Castle,* referred to as 'the lower animals' as well as four or five human skeletons and 'some coins of the lower empire' (Colt Hoare 1812, 123).

There has been much debate as to why the Cup was in the well. Most eighteenth and nineteenth century antiquaries appear to have presumed that the whole assemblage was a votive offering. This idea was particularly popular after the discovery of Coventina's Well, at Carrawburgh on Hadrian's Wall, in the 1870s, although it is worth mentioning that John Collingwood Bruce, who as the local authority on Hadrian's Wall in the nineteenth century had been very much involved in the analysis of the contents of Coventina's Well, scorned this suggestion when writing his catalogue of the Duke of Northumberland's collection:

> The idea was long entertained that the cup had been thrown into the well as an offering to the nymph who presided over its waters. The bones and human skeletons cannot have been presented as an act of devotion to the goddess. The cup had probably come there by accident, or was thrown in for concealment.
>
> (Bruce 1880, 139)

John Cowen and Sir Ian Richmond were of the same opinion, stating that 'There is nothing whatever to suggest that the well was invested with any sacred character, while the presence of the animals' bones argues strongly against it. How the cup found its way into the well we shall never know, nor, with the votive idea once disposed of, are we much concerned!' (Cowen and Richmond 1935, 313). They went on to comment that 'the absence of other articles of value of anything like comparable date seems to rule out the hypothesis of intentional concealment. It may, of course, represent an accidental loss such as might happen at any time and any place. More picturesque, however, and on the whole more likely, is the possibility that it went down concealed on the person of one of those unfortunate skeletons, whose presence in such a place can be attributed only to a scene of violence'.

ON ITS WAY TO ALNWICK

So how did the Cup travel from Wiltshire to Alnwick and to the possession of the Duke of Northumberland? This is a complex tale worthy of Charles Dickens.

The first of the Percy family to arrive in England from Normandy was Alan de Percy, some years before the Norman Conquest. The family prospered and became famous, not least through the works of William Shakespeare. In the early seventeenth century the family's fortunes became less firm. The Tenth Earl of Northumberland, one Algernon Percy, married twice, the first time to a Cecil. His father disapproved of this liaison saying firmly that 'the blood of a Percy would not mix with the blood of a Cecil if you poured it on a dish' (Drake 2004-7). The marriage produced five daughters but no sons. After his first wife died he married again and produced one son, Josceline later the Eleventh Earl, who in turn produced a son who died in infancy. The male line died out with Josceline – the only true Percy surviving in the direct line being his daughter Lady Elizabeth Percy who was described as the 'loneliest and richest heiress in the country' when her father died, when she was four years old, in 1670. She was obviously very eligible and as such was married three times before she was 16. At the age of 12 she was married to the Earl of Ogle who died after six months. Her second husband was Thomas Thynne of Longleat who was murdered in Pall Mall by assassins hired by Count Konigsmark, who wished to be her third husband. His plan, however, failed and in 1682 she married the Duke of Somerset; this was not the happiest of marriages as the Duke had a reputation as an overbearing tyrant whose sanity was questionable. When she died in 1722, all her Percy estates were absorbed by the dukedom of Somerset and her son Algernon Seymour was created Baron Percy to protect the inheritance. It was Algernon Seymour who held the title of Earl of Hertford and discovered the Rudge Cup. In some publications there is some confusion as to the identity of the excavator, but Algernon Seymour, the Earl of Hertford and the Seventh Duke of Somerset were all one and the same person.

Algernon married Frances Thynne and had a son, Lord Beauchamp, and a daughter, also called Elizabeth who, in 1740, married a Yorkshire squire called Sir Hugh Smithson. When her brother died Elizabeth found herself the only heir of the Seymours as well as the only heir of the Percys. Her husband was created Earl of Northumberland and later Duke of Northumberland. As part of her inheritance she took possession of Alnwick Castle, Northumberland House and Syon House, and with them the Rudge Cup.

The Cup having passed to Elizabeth, it might be presumed that it was placed in a cupboard or on a shelf for display. However, the noble families of England in the eighteenth century tended to have several houses and many possessions and it is a fact that things go missing in even the best regulated households. The Rudge Cup appears to have been ignored, to the extent that after its publication by John Horsley in *Britannia Romana* in 1732, it was thought to be missing by the archaeological community for many years. Colt Hoare, in his publication of 1812, was happy to state that it was in the Duke of Northumberland's possession but did not specify at which ducal property. There is some doubt whether he saw the object himself as 'traces of its preservation had for some time been lost' when Albert Way, an antiquary who was friendly with the 4th Duke, noticed it during a visit to Northumberland House in London (Way 1857; Way 1859). He arranged for it to be included in the exhibition being prepared in Edinburgh in July 1856 for the visit of the Archaeological Institute to the city. It then followed the Institute back to its London headquarters and was the subject of a lecture by Albert Way on 1 May 1857.

Albert Way did much work on the Duke's archaeological collection and seems to have been the guiding force behind the formation of a Museum of Antiquities in one of the towers at Alnwick Castle. It was due to him that the Rudge Cup was included in the Museum's display and there it remains.

The Rudge Cup is a small object that spends most of its time these days sitting quietly in the Duke's museum at Alnwick Castle. Visitors seeing it there rarely have any idea of its importance to our Roman heritage or that it is the one object that is invariably mentioned in any publication about military frontiers, Hadrian's Wall or Roman Britain.

It has been studied by a remarkable range of people. Indeed, the list reads like a Who's Who of European Archaeology: the Earl of Hertford with his links to the Society of Antiquaries of London, Albert Way and his display and lecture to the members of the Archaeological Institute, John Horsley, the learned Gale , Sir Richard Colt Hoare, Françoise Henry, John Cowen, Sir Ian Richmond and all those scholars who have used the Cup as evidence for crenellations on Hadrian s Wall. Anybody who is anybody in Wall studies seems to have expressed an opinion on the Rudge Cup.

Whether it is agreed that the Cup shows crenellations, has a mid-second century date or comes from a British workshop, it is certainly beyond question that the Rudge Cup has more than played its part in the archaeology of Roman Britain in this last 280 years of its life. The interest shown in it now would be quite a shock to the person who first made it as a souvenir or the person, soldier or civilian, man or woman, who bought it.

Chapter 4
The Amiens Patera

Noel Maheo

The Amiens Patera was discovered in 1949 at the junction of the rue des trois cailloux and the rue Robert de Luzarches in the town of that name. It was found by Françoise Vasselle in a Gallo-Roman house with a hypocaust and a small bath together with a pipeclay figurine of a mother goddess; it was classified as a historic monument and work of art in 1950. The vessel was deposited by the state in the Museum of Picardy, Amiens (inv. 3984). The *patera* 'contenant 4 anneaux de bronze et des boutons (?)' [four bronze rings and some possible stud heads] (Vasselle 1949/50, 236).

The *patera* is of bronze with enamel colouring, with a height of 56mm and a diameter of 100mm; the length of the handle was 90mm (Figures 1.2, 4.1).

This precious object, with a separately-worked handle fixed to the bowl after manufacture, is decorated with champlevé enamel, a technique involving hollowing the metal base to create cavities for receiving the enamel, a vitreous material that is coloured, melted and then hardened. The *patera* lists six forts in the western sector of Hadrian's Wall:

MAIS/ABALLAVA/VXELLODVNVM/CAMBOGLẠ[NI]S/BANNA/
ESICA

Maia (Bowness-on-Solway), *Aballava* (Burgh-by-Sands), *Uxelodunum* (Stanwix), *Camboglanna* (Castlesteads), *Banna* (Birdoswald), *Aesica* (Great Chesters)

The names are picked out in red and are placed on a background which is alternatively blue and green, each fort having its own colour.

Below the inscription, on the bowl, a red crenellated line figuratively depicts a wall and seven towers, each one formed of four adjacent rectangles that are alternately blue and green, and which depict the stones, the base being decorated with a checkerboard pattern of rectangles that are similarly blue and green, giving the impression of a masonry foundation. It appears to be a contemporary representation of Hadrian's Wall, 118km long, protected by towers and 17 forts. A road, the *via militaris*, was created to connect the forts and it is that road that is depicted on the Amiens Patera, with its six fort names of the western sector of the Wall.

A travelling legionary who came to Amiens (*Samarobriva*), leading a

Figure 4.1. The Amiens Patera, a. MAISABALLAVAVXEL[;
b. VXELODVNVMCAMBOGL[; c. CAMBOG[   ]SBANNA; d. BANNAESICAMAISABALL[

Figure 4.2. The handle on the Amiens Patera

peaceful life after having been granted leave must have lost this souvenir of war that was given to the soldiers of the *limes*. Amiens was a stopping place for soldiers, as is confirmed by the epitaph on the funerary stone of a legionary leaving for an expedition to Britain at the beginning of the third century (Museum of Picardy inv. 1876.223 = *CIL* XIII 3496), while the town has also produced the tombstone of a senior officer (*primus pilus*) of the Sixth Legion which was based in Britain (*CIL* XIII 3497).

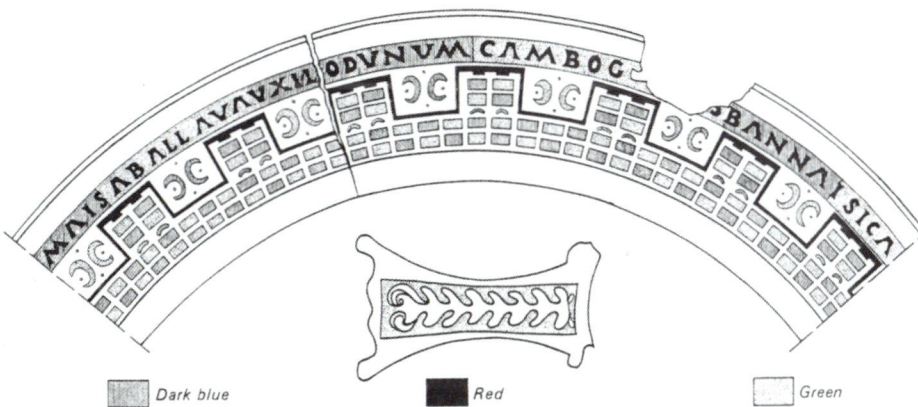

Figure 4.3. The Amiens Patera (Heurgon, 1952)

Chapter 5

The Ilam Pan

Ralph Jackson

INTRODUCTION

This inscribed and flamboyantly-enamelled small bronze vessel was unearthed by metal-detectorists in June 2003. It was promptly and correctly reported to staff of the Portable Antiquities Scheme who drew the attention of relevant museums to the find. In 2005, with the substantial and generous support of the Heritage Lottery Fund, the pan was jointly acquired by the British Museum, London (2005, 1204.1. PRN BCB127984), the Potteries Museum and Art Gallery, Stoke-on-Trent (STKMG: 2006.LH1) and the Tullie House Museum and Gallery, Carlisle (CALMG: 2006.1) (Jackson 2005). Since August 2005 it has been displayed consecutively at all three venues in a rolling annual cycle, interrupted from January to May 2008, when it was lent to South Shields Museum for a special display, and June 2009 to April 2010, when it was returned to Carlisle out of sequence in order to coincide with the Pilgrimage of Hadrian's Wall. In the absence of the original pan each museum has the possibility to display an exact replica, three of which were made by the British Museum's replication specialist in 2005.

At the time of discovery and throughout the lengthy acquisition process the precise find spot of the pan was not made public, in deference to the wishes of the finders and landowners, and the provenance was given as 'Staffordshire Moorlands'. Thus, as the subject of considerable media and academic interest the pan became known as The Staffordshire Moorlands Pan or simply The Staffordshire Pan. While it is frequently still referred to by those names its more precise provenance, Ilam, Staffordshire – already disclosed in Roger Tomlin's initial assessment of the inscription in *Britannia* in 2004 – is now in general use.

DISCOVERY

The pan was discovered by Kevin Blackburn and his fellow detectorist Julian Lee, on the last Sunday in June 2003. They were part of a group of friends on a regular metal detecting weekend searching farmland with the permission of the landowner. The site, on sloping elevated moorland within an area of former lead-mining, overlooks the valley of the River Manifold.

This is a rather remarkable river since for several miles in this sector it disappears underground, except when in spate, before re-appearing at the 'boil holes' near Ilam Hall, where it joins, and assumes the name of, the River Dove. Responding to a strong metal-detector signal Blackburn found the pan about a foot beneath the surface, upright, with its rim protruding from beneath a block of limestone (Pitts and Worrell 2003, 22-4). The fine state of preservation of the pan left them in no doubt as to its identification and importance and the following morning they contacted Jane Stewart, Portable Antiquities Scheme Finds Liaison Officer for Staffordshire and the West Midlands, who had been meeting them regularly to record a steady stream of their finds. Stewart notified Deborah Ford (now Klemperer), Collections Officer (Local History) at the Potteries Museum and Art Gallery, Stoke-on-Trent. Subsequently Bill Klemperer, Staffordshire County Archaeologist, and Ken Smith, Archaeologist for the Peak District National Park, visited the site to assess the context of the find spot. Their consensus was that the pan and other artefacts found nearby were obviously of interest, but there did not appear to be evidence of any associated archaeological features. The pan was also incomplete and damaged at the time of deposition – the finders had searched carefully for the missing base-plate and handle but there were no directly associated objects or other detectable artefacts in the immediate vicinity. Unassociated objects found nearby include several Roman coins, ranging in date from a Republican *denarius* of 80 BC to fourth-century issues, an enamelled stud, a 'dumbbell' toggle and a lead spindle whorl, as well as Anglo-Saxon and later medieval artefacts. More particularly, a relatively large number of brooches – at least 12 – were found, several of which were reported to have been orientated in the same direction, seemingly in some sort of extended linear arrangement. All are of first to second century date, comprising Polden Hill, Headstud and Trumpet types, and most are complete or nearly so.

Description

The pan, which has lost its handle and base-plate, comprises a small circular bowl of copper alloy inscribed and inlaid with champlevé polychrome enamel. The bowl is damaged but otherwise complete, with a simple small beaded rim, convex wall and slightly-flared raised foot-ring, externally rebated to accommodate the base-plate. At two points the top of the wall is heavily dented inwards, in one case with associated splitting at the base of the rim, in the other with a corresponding distortion of the foot-ring to a sub-oval shape. A zone of differential corrosion and decayed solder in an arc immediately beneath the rim (Figure 5.1) discloses both the former position of the handle – above the inscribed lettering SCOGGABATAVXELO – and its width at the point of contact with the bowl – *c.* 68mm, measured along the chord.

Similar corrosion products are visible in the rebated foot-ring. In accordance with surviving complete pans of this form, the handle would probably have been of flat bow-tie shape, with enamel inlay on the upper surface (Figure 5.7), the base-plate a turned or plain metal disc.

Figure 5.1. The Ilam Pan. An arc of decayed solder below the rim reveals the position of the handle. MAIS COGGABATA. Roundels 1 and 2

Interim results from preliminary scientific investigation (non-destructive surface analysis), by Duncan Hook of the British Museum's Department of Conservation and Scientific Research, indicate 1) that the body metal of the pan is a leaded bronze and 2) that enhanced tin and lead levels correspond to the remains of soft solder at areas under the rim (handle attachment) and within the foot-ring (base plate attachment).

a. Dimensions

Maximum diameter (on line of inscription)	94mm
Original external rim diameter	*c.* 90mm
Original base external diameter	*c.* 54mm
Height	47mm
Weight	132.5g
Capacity	*c.* 160ml

b. Inscription

The greater part of the wall of the pan is occupied by a zone of colourful decoration. Above the decoration is a slender cambered band which encircles the bowl at its point of maximum diameter. Into this narrow but prominent field was engraved a Latin inscription (Figure 5.4). It consists of an unbroken and unpunctuated sequence of 56 capital letters, the A's blind, that is without the central bar. The letters, mostly about 4mm high (within the range 3.5-4.5mm) and quite deeply cut, were engraved beneath a single discontinuous incised guideline and then inlaid with enamel. A sequence of nine letters – MAISCOGGA – preserves the enamel virtually intact (Figure 5.1) and traces are present in all of the remaining letters: in every case the colour is identifiable as turquoise.

The inscription reads:

MAISCOGGABATAVXELODVNVMCAMMOGIANNARIGOREVALIA
ELIDRACONIS

That is:

MAIS (Bowness-on-Solway) COGGABATA (Drumburgh)
VXELODVNVM (Stanwix) CAMMOGIANNA (Castlesteads)
RIGORE VALI AELI DRACONIS

Figure 5.2. The Ilam Pan. VXELODVNVM CAMMOGIANNA. Roundels 3, 4, 5

The lettering is simply and competently rendered, with an occasional vestigial serif, and the spacing is comparatively even (I mistakenly cut for L in CAMMOGIANNA and an over-generous space between the E and L of VXELODVNVM are the exceptions). Nevertheless, there is some variation and the relative density provides clues as to the sequence and relationship of the inscribed words. To the extent that at the time the pan was inscribed and used the meaning of the various parts of the inscription were probably readily understood by literate viewers, the beginning and precise sequence probably did not matter, but clearly they are important today above all in seeking to clarify which words belong with which in the sequence RIGORE VALI AELI DRACONIS. Following a close study of the inscription and citing letter size and relative spacing between letters and words, Tomlin (Tomlin and Hassall 2004, 344-5) has argued a case for the 'start' of the inscription at the word RIGORE, having rejected the 'logical' start (with reference to the Rudge and Amiens inscriptions) at MAIS.

Figure 5.3. The Ilam Pan. RIGORE VALI AELI DRACONIS. Roundels 6, 7, 8

However, an alternative sequence may be proposed: the word that appears to have been given greatest prominence both in terms of letter size and spacing as well as in position – optimal for viewing by a right-handed user – is DRACONIS, and it is conceivable that this was the first inscribed word. This would be very appropriate, given that Draco(n) is almost certainly to be identified as the owner of the pan who bought it and then commissioned and specified the inscribed wording. It is far less likely that Draco was the maker of the pan – makers' marks on metalwork were generally stamped. One could then argue that a suitable space was left after DRACONIS before engraving MAIS and a slightly more minimal spacing provided between the subsequent fort names. Then, having squandered a space between E and L in VXELODVNVM the craftsman may have realised as he completed the last fort name that he was running short of space and hence not only left virtually no separation between CAMMOGIANNA and RIGORE but reduced and compressed the lettering of RIGORE sufficiently to allow the return of 'normal' spacing and separation for the remaining two words VALI AELI.

c. Ornament

The inlaid decoration on the wall of the pan comprises a frieze of colourful Celtic-style curvilinear ornament, the vibrancy and fluidity of which is adapted to, and significantly enhanced by, the vertical and horizontal curvature of

Figure 5.4. The Ilam Pan. Periphery photograph

the field it occupies. The frieze comprises a symmetrical arrangement of eight contiguous roundels interspersed with eight 'hour-glass' motifs, an integrated design which incorporates elements of reserved metal but depends principally for its effect on the inlays of coloured enamel.

For clarity in the following account the roundels are referred to as numbers 1 to 8, starting with that beneath the word MAIS and running with the inscription from left to right (counter-clockwise) to finish with the roundel beneath the word DRACONIS. All the roundels are based on the same design but they are in no sense a repeating pattern. Thus, while they have an overall uniform appearance no two are identical, either in decor or in size: none is truly circular and all are of variable overall dimensions, ranging between 28 and 35mm wide and between 30 and 34mm high.

Each roundel encloses a counter-clockwise-swirling whirligig composed of three commas interspersed with a triskele centred on a tiny three-petalled device, a combination well suited to the confines of a roundel and with a long history. It can, for example, be paralleled on metalwork as far back as the La Tène Developed Style, as on a three-cornered whorl on the interior of the bronze basin from Les Saulces Champénoise (Harding 2007, 70-1, fig. 4.5, 2). The repeating trio of tri-partite motifs (3 x 3) on the Ilam roundels suggests, at first sight, a conscious incorporation of multiples of the powerful number three. However, any theory of an integrated overall scheme based on the power of three may be decisively rejected by the fact that the frieze comprises not nine (or six) but eight roundels interspersed with eight 'hour-glass' motifs: the concept of the frieze was purely decorative and the size of the roundels was to a great extent dictated by the circumference of the pan and the chosen height of the frieze. An alternative symmetry is suggested by the fact that the number of roundels corresponds to the number of words in the inscription. However, the latter vary in length to a far greater degree than the variation in diameter of the roundels preventing any meaningful synchronicity.

In the present state of the pan the most prominent feature of the roundels is the outermost swirling 'comma' motif, a disintegrated version of the interlocking 'comma pairs' ("yin yangs") or 'triple comma whorls' contrived as roundel motifs, which were a long-standing part of the repertoire of Celtic art (see e.g. Harding 2007, fig. 4.4, 4, fig. 4.5, 2, fig. 7.5, 7-8) and these commas are seen again near the top of the complicated design on the large enamelled plaque in the form of an altar found in the River Thames at London (Smith 1922, 95 and pl. IX left; Brailsford 1964, 56, no. 3 and pl. XXI, 3) (Figure 5.5). However, the comma motif is also related to the 'fin', the basic design motif of the majority of British Iron Age mirrors (Jope 2000, 381; Joy 2010, 25-6), and the Ilam scheme may be interpreted as a development of 'mirror style' (Jody Joy *pers. comm.*). In every case the Ilam trio of plump elongated commas comprises two inlaid with blue enamel and one inlaid with turquoise.

Figure 5.5. Enamelled plaque in the form of an altar from the River Thames at London

Generally the arrangement is blue at base and left with turquoise at right, but in two cases (roundels 1 and 4) the roundel design was rotated slightly clockwise resulting in blue at left and top and turquoise at right. In just one instance (roundel 1) the upper edge of the upper blue-inlaid comma has a three-toothed serration which impinges on the narrow space beneath the inscribed lettering (Figure 5.6). This feature matches a similar provision at the top edge of each of the intervening 'hour-glass' motifs. Similarly, the incorporation in

Figure 5.6. The Ilam Pan. Rectified photograph of Roundel 1

the two idiosyncratic blue-inlaid commas of a simple pendant tendril of reserved metal also corresponds to the inclusion of that feature in the upper part of the 'hour-glass' motif. All the other commas, whether inlaid with blue or turquoise enamel, incorporate a more elaborate tripartite forked tendril of reserved metal, closely paralleled by the commas on the Thames 'altar' plaque (Figure 5.5). These tendrils, while no doubt primarily decorative, may have had a secondary, more functional, purpose since they effectively divided up the areas of enamel, perhaps as a means of avoiding the instability of a broad uninterrupted expanse of inlay.

The central framework that interlocked with the commas and gave pace to the roundel design was a symmetrical swirling triskele. Its crescent-shaped legs were inlaid with coloured enamel and, in common with other parts of the decorative frieze, their concave edge was serrated. Although the enamel inlay remains largely intact, in most legs of the triskeles its colour appears to have degraded and is often indeterminate. In only one instance (roundel 8) is it possible to suggest that all three legs appear to have contained red enamel. Thus, while it is likely that red was universally applied to all parts of all the triskeles, the variety of surface colour in the present state of the enamel inlays – in particular a lilac/purple-grey surface colouring in one or more of the triskele legs in roundels 1-7 – encourages caution.

A similar uncertainty attaches to the inlay colour of the third and final component, the tiny triple-petalled device at the eye of the roundel. All three petals are part-filled with a cream-coloured vitreous-looking substance which, in one or two places, appears to retain its surface. Although this suggests the original colour may actually have been a shade of cream or pale yellow there is reason to question that. For, what appears to be the same cream-coloured substance can be seen in the hollow-sided triangles of the 'hour-glass' motif, where it seems to be a substrate of both the red and the turquoise enamel and is most clearly exposed in those cells which have lost the greater part of the surface of their enamel, principally the red. It is thus possible that the enamel colour of the petals was originally red or turquoise.

The eight interspersed 'hour-glass' motifs, effectively the background to the roundels, consist of opposing pairs of hollow-sided triangles, the lower one slightly smaller than the upper because of the curvature of the bowl. The visual effect is of an upper and a lower row of triangles (each triangle equating to a conjoined (back-to-back) pair of spandrels). The intention appears to have been to alternate red and turquoise enamel in both rows of triangles and to offset the sequence so that there was also a red/ turquoise contrast for each vertical pair. That regular arrangement can be seen in the lower row, but in two of the triangles of the upper row (between roundels 1/2 and 7/8) it appears that turquoise inlay was inadvertently inserted in place of red. Thus, instead of interspersed red and turquoise the result is: t, **t**, t, r, t, r, t, **t**.

In the upper row the turquoise inlays have survived quite well, with four remaining intact or nearly so (1/2, 4/5, 6/7, 8/1) and vestiges in the other two (2/3, 7/8). The red has fared much worse, with only a tiny fragment in 5/6 and no colouration at all in 3/4. Similarly, in the lower row all four turquoise inlays are intact (1/2, 3/4, 5/6, 7/8), while of the red inlays only fragments survive in two cells (2/3, 8/1) and the other two are completely devoid of colour (4/5, 6/7).

The eight triangular cells of the upper row incorporate a single comma-like tendril of reserved metal which descends from their top edge. In each instance, on the top edge of the triangle to the left of the tendril stem, there are four serrated 'teeth', similar to the serrated edges of some of the roundel motifs. In all cases the serrations contain enamel inlay. In the case of triangle 6/7 the serrations actually encroach on the lower edge of the inscription (the letters VAL of VALI) or, more probably, the inscription impinged on the serrations.

Most of the eight cells of the lower row of triangles incorporate a simple stem/ tendril of reserved metal which rises from the centre of the bottom edge, but this feature is absent from turquoise cell 7/8 and the (empty) red cells 4/5 and 6/7. There are no serrations on the lower (smaller) row of triangles.

Clearly the balance between the wall thickness of the pan and the depth of the inlaid cells was critical and in general it seems to have been successfully achieved. In one place, however – the 'tail' of the turquoise comma in roundel 4 – a tiny area of the metal backing of the cell was breached and filled with enamel, which can be seen as a turquoise speck on the pan's inner surface. This small flaw is unlikely to have compromised the functionality of the pan which would still likely have been watertight and which is unlikely to have been intended to be subject to intense heat.

The state of preservation of the enamel inlay in the various components of the design may be indicative of different enamel compositions and/or variation in colours or shades of colour. Most uniform in appearance, and seemingly retaining their original colour, are the blue and turquoise enamel inlays in the roundel 'commas', almost all of which are virtually intact with a translucent or semi-translucent, 'glassy' appearance and a more or less crackled or crazed surface. Identical in appearance, though slightly less complete, is the turquoise enamel inlay in the upper and lower components of the 'hour-glass' motif – eight out of ten are intact and just two lack much of their inlay and reveal a cream-coloured vitreous-looking substrate. Very similar, too, if a shade 'greener', is the appearance of the turquoise enamel inlay in the inscribed lettering, though, perhaps surprisingly, preservation is less good with only a few letters (MAISCOGGA) preserving near-intact inlays.

Much more fugitive is the red enamel inlay in the upper and lower triangular components of the 'hour-glass' motif in which very little of the original surface survives. The tiny remaining enamel fragments are bright red with an underlying cream-coloured vitreous-looking substrate. Very different in appearance, both in colour and in texture, is the reddish-coloured enamel inlay in the legs of the triskeles in the roundels. The colour is more opaque and 'paste-like' than that in the 'hour-glass' triangles and the enamel often deeply-fissured, split, surface-depleted or eroded. While the original colour of the enamel inlay in all the triskele legs was most probably red, now at different stages of decomposition, the variety of appearance both within and across the roundels at least raises the possibility of different shades of red.

In summary, the polychrome effect of the pan's decor appears to have depended upon a symmetrical integrated design of red, blue and turquoise inlays set off against the golden-coloured background and detailing of the reserved copper-alloy body metal.

DISCUSSION

Roman enamelled bronze vessels were commonly of composite construction, with panels and components riveted together, like the hexagonal vase in the Rheinisches Landesmuseum, Bonn (Henry 1933, 143, pl. II) or, more often, joined with soft tin-lead solder – seen most dramatically in the eight-component 'Ambleteuse Vase' in the British Museum (1843, 0623.1. Henry 1933, 143 and fig. 45, 1), recently identified as a *clepsydra* or wine-lifter (Bailey 2003, 4-7, figs 1.5 and 1.6). As the joins were potential weak points, those

Figure 5.7. The Braughing Pan (right) with an un-provenanced handle and a replica of the Rudge Cup

vessels that survive are frequently incomplete and much more commonly found are single stray panels or components (e.g. handle from Scole, Norfolk (Rogerson 1977, 140-2) and vase panels from Silchester (Henry 1933, fig. 46, 2) and Sutton, Suffolk (PAS SF10415) (Figures 8.6 and 8.7).

The Ilam pan belongs to a series of small colourful enamelled bronze pans dating from the late first to third centuries (Moore 1978). Their tripartite construction comprised bowl, base-plate and handle joined with solder (Figure 5.7). Several have retained their handle and a few have remained completely intact – as in the case of the examples from West Lothian (Hunter, this volume) (Figure 9.1) and Bad Pyrmont (Henry 1933, 122, fig. 30, 4 and fig. 32, 1; Müller 2002, 83-8 and fig. 56) (Figure 2.6) which came to be termed respectively skillet and *patère* – but those lacking a handle have often been described as a bowl or cup. As Moore long since observed (1978, 319), however, the Braughing pan (Franks 1870; Potter 1983, fig. 63) – like the Ilam pan and others – preserves traces of the solder that secured its now missing handle, and it is probable that all of these small pans were originally handled. The remains of the solder on the bowl of those pans that had lost their handle and base-plate would be very vulnerable to the stabilisation, cleaning or removal of corrosion products that many of the pre-modern finds are likely to have undergone at some point following their discovery. So, for example, we should not be surprised that it is not now possible to discern any solder on the rim or base-seating of the Rudge Cup (Allason-Jones, this volume). The solder is most clearly seen on the pan from the Bath sacred spring (Figure 5.10), the anaerobic conditions of which, while not conducive to the survival of the enamel inlay, preserved the bronze pan particularly well, and the grey-coloured solder securing handle and base-plate is clearly visible against the gold-coloured body metal (Brown 1988, 14-16, fig. 8, no. 23, pl. X).

These small handled pans very likely correspond to a diminutive version of the ancient *trulla* (Strong 1966, 130; Hilgers 1969, 291-3, no. 364) and they probably should not be called *patera*, a type of vessel which (at least in the ancient usage of the word) was not equipped with a handle (Boon 1988, 525; Frere and Tomlin 1991, 44). Nor is the use of the pre-modern 'skillet' particularly helpful, with its implication of feet. Thus, in view of the uncertainty over their precise ancient nomenclature (see, for example, the brief discussion of the identity of the *trullae* listed in two of the Vindolanda Writing Tablets (194. B. 6; 596. ii. 15, 16, 17: Bowman and Thomas 1994, 162-5; Bowman and Thomas 2003, 55-8), and to avoid potentially confusing modern terminology, it seems preferable to use the simple objective words 'small handled pan' or 'small pan'.

The majority of these small pans have decorative schemes based either on alternating friezes or on interlocking panels of stylised vegetal ornament inlaid with coloured enamel. Moore (1978, 320-1) characterised these as

West Lothian Type (Group B) and, following Eggers (1966, 94), Vehner Moor Type (Group C). Both groups feature a fine concave moulding below the rim, beneath which Group B bowls are ornamented with three horizontal registers, the uppermost a stylised wreath, the middle a vine scroll and the lower a vandyked border – a 'toothed' band of elongated triangles (Figure 5.8). Group C has a more vertical arrangement of interlocking pentagons and triangles enclosing a variety of leaf and scroll motifs. The enamel colours most commonly comprise red, blue and green (or turquoise), with red being used frequently in both groups to delineate or emphasise the border between friezes and panels. On those examples which retain their handle, the design and decorative motifs tend to reflect in part those on the bowl. Thus, the ivy-leaf and tendril motif on the handle of the Group C Bad Pyrmont pan references that on its bowl as does, to a lesser extent, that of the Group B West Lothian pan (Hunter, this volume) (Figures 2.6 and 9.1).

Figure 5.8. The Braughing Pan

Two pans and one fragment – Moore's Rudge Type (Group A) – stand out from the series: the Rudge Cup, found in the filling of a well at a Roman villa at Rudge Coppice, Froxfield, near Marlborough, Wiltshire in 1725, the Amiens Patera, found in a Gallo-Roman building adjacent to the forum at Amiens in 1949 and the Hildburgh Fragment, found in unknown circumstances before 1935, probably between León and Zamora in northern Spain. They have a near-identical décor consisting of what has been identified (Cowen and Richmond 1935, 317-8) as a stylised mural frieze, complete with crenellation or turrets, seven in number, surmounted by an encircling inscription, all in bronze relief on an enamelled background (the Hildburgh Fragment does not preserve any lettering). The inscriptions list the names of forts in the western sector of Hadrian's Wall, and the 'mural' motif has been interpreted as a schematic representation of the Wall itself, with its regularly-spaced turrets (or, perhaps more likely, in view of the overlying inscription, the northern gateway of forts attached to the Wall).

The 36 letters of the Rudge Cup inscription record five forts, MAIS (Bowness-on-Solway), ABALLAVA (Burgh-by-Sands), VXELODVM (Stanwix), CAMBOGLANS (Castlesteads) and BANNA (Birdoswald). The 40 (originally 43) letters of the Amiens Patera repeat these forts (varying only in the spelling of Stanwix – VXELODVNVM and, probably, Castlesteads – CAMBOGLA[NI]S) but add a sixth, ESICA (Great Chesters). The form, size and spacing of the lettering on both vessels are near-identical and it is possible that they were the product of a set of individual letter stamps, of common origin if not in the same workshop. Most distinctive is the combination of blind A's, bold triangular serifs and heavily squared-off angles of the A's and V's. Unlike the relief-cast lettering of the Rudge Cup the inscription of the Amiens Patera has been described as 'moulded in red letters' (Heurgon 1951, 22) and 'se détache en rouge' (Maheo 1990, 266), implying that the letters are picked out in red enamel. However, it is possible that this is a surface discolouration, a consequence of its fire damage, rather than inlay and it is matched by the same discolouration of the reserved copper-alloy body metal elsewhere on the pan.

The Ilam inscription is no mere repeat of the Rudge and Amiens examples. At 56 letters it is substantially longer and it comprises two parts. 34 letters list just four forts, but one, COGGABATA, is an addition. Following MAIS it is evidently the fort at Drumburgh (*Congavata*), an important confirmation of Rivet's identification (Rivet and Smith 1979, 315), though perhaps with a more accurate spelling, and it fills the gap between MAIS and ABALLAVA on the Rudge/Amiens inscriptions. Still more significant are the remaining 22 letters of the inscription – RIGORE VALI AELI DRACONIS. The first ten letters, if interpreted as a pair of words, would appear to be a direct reference to Hadrian's Wall itself, referred to in antiquity as 'the vallum', as, for example, on the Kirksteads altar (*RIB* I 2034) – 'ob res trans vallum prospere gestas' – and in the *Notitia Dignitatum* (*Occ.* 40. 32) – 'per lineam valli' (Figure 5.9). The remaining 12 letters may form the personal name Aelius Draco (or Dracon), most likely that of the man the pan was made for, perhaps a soldier or official who served on the Wall. Alternatively, and perhaps more convincingly, Tomlin and Hassall (2004, 345) suggested that 'Aeli' may belong with the preceding words '*rigore vali*', thus specifying 'along

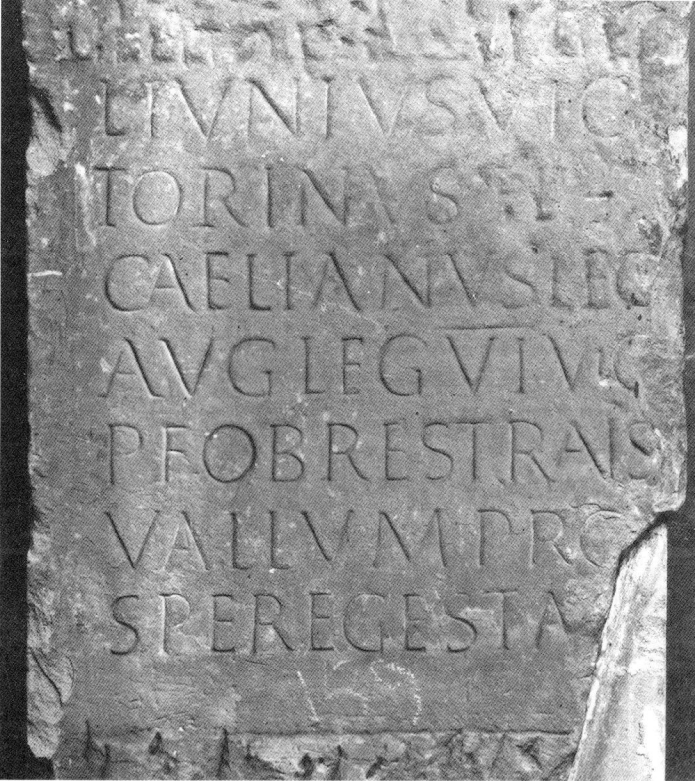

Figure 5.9. The Kirksteads Altar (*RIB* I, 2034. BM 1970, 0102.6), detail of inscribed panel

the wall of Aelius' (i.e. Hadrian). Whether attached to 'Draco' or to '*rigore vali*' the *nomen* Aelius, as the *gentilicium* of the emperor Hadrian (Publius Aelius Hadrianus), is clearly significant for the dating of the vessel. Taking the evidence of the inscription, the pan is most likely to have been made after the addition of forts to the Wall and either before the move north to the Antonine Wall, i.e. *c*. 125/140 (Tomlin and Hassall 2004, 345), or (though less likely) to the decades following the 're-activation' of Hadrian's Wall as Britain's northern frontier in the 160s. A date within either bracket is consistent with the wider evidence for the *floruit* of production of enamelled bronzes in Britain.

The enamel inlay backing the lettering on the Rudge Cup is now missing, but it probably corresponded to that on the Amiens Patera which preserves sufficient to show that the background to the inscription comprised interspersed panels of blue and green enamel (Heurgon 1951, 22; Maheo 1990, 266), highlighting the individual fort names and thus obviating the need for interpunct or separation. Indeed, the fort names of the Rudge Cup could even have followed the same colour sequence, its preposition A providing the necessary sixth unit, complementing the 'extra' fort name – ESICA – of the Amiens inscription. The Ilam inscription shares the blind A feature but is otherwise substantially different. While the striking – even gaudy – visual effect of the Rudge and Amiens inscriptions would have been a golden-coloured or red text backed by interspersed panels of bright blue and vivid green that highlighted the different fort names, that of Ilam would have been a reversed and slightly more restrained colour contrast with turquoise lettering on a golden-coloured backing and only the viewer's knowledge or degree of literacy as an aid to separating and identifying the individual fort names and other components of the inscription.

One of the distinguishing features of the Rudge Type pans is a convex band below the rim, in place of the concave moulding of Moore's Groups B and C. This feature is shared with the pans from Bath, Beadlam, Bingen and Winterton (Figures 1.5 and 8.1) as well as that from Ilam and may imply a common workshop tradition, for all are linked to the Rudge Type in other ways too: the Ilam pan by its inscription, the Bath pan by its mural frieze and the Bingen and Winterton pans by their chequerboard design – clearly related to the 'coursed masonry' lower border of the Rudge Type. The pan fragment from Beadlam comprises part of the wall of the bowl, with a relief-cast inscription, and although the surviving letters are not identifiable as a Hadrian's Wall fort name (*RIB* II. 2, 2415.54) they are in the same position and of the same size, style and spacing as the Rudge and Amiens lettering. Furthermore, there is another potential linkage: the Beadlam wall decoration, a symmetrical looped meander with pale blue enamel backing, is paralleled by a similar 'scrolled' motif on the enamelled handle of the Amiens pan (compare Heurgon 1951, fig. 4 with *RIB* II. 2, 2415.54).

However, other indicators suggest a 'pick and mix' approach for these small handled pans from a common pool of stylistic traits and motifs, which are found in different combinations and permutations across Moore's Groups and in other enamelled products. Thus, for example, vandyked borders are found on Group B pans from West Lothian, Braughing and Maltbœk, on the Group A Hildburgh Fragment and on many other contemporary British enamelled bronzes, including cosmetic sets (Jackson 2010, 24-5) and miniature stands (Bird 2007, fig. 22, no. 82. Henig 1984, fig. 53), while red enamel was commonly selected for the linear border dividing friezes or panels, whether on Group A (Rudge and Amiens), Group B (West Lothian) or Group C (Rochefort) pans, as, too, on some of the miniature stands (Bird 2007, fig. 23, no. 83) and on the Thames plaque. Still more ubiquitous is the selective 'nicked' or 'serrated' edging of enamelled fields, seen on the pans from Rudge, Amiens, Bath, Beadlam, West Lothian, Braughing, Maltbæk, Rochefort, Canterbury and Ilam, and on the Hildburgh Fragment, which probably doubled as a pleasing motif in its own right and an 'anchor' for the enamel. Even in the small Rudge Group there is variety: blocks, crescents and meander on the Rudge and Amiens pans; blocks, petals, meander and leaves on the Bath pan; and blocks, petals, meander, scroll and vandyking on the larger Hildburgh vessel (see Table 1.1).

Similarly varied is the decor of the handles on the few remaining complete pans: the decoration of the handle of the Amiens pan is independent of that on its bowl, in contrast to the integrated decoration of bowl and handle on the complete pans of Moore's Types B and C; and the Rudge variant pan from Bath, too, preserves sufficient of its handle to demonstrate that its design and decor were different to those of its bowl. In each case discovery of the handle alone would provide no clue as to the nature of the bowl decor. Thus, in theory at least, handles such as those from Brough-on-Fosse and Burgh Apton (Moore 1978, figs. 1 and 4) might have been attached to Rudge-type pans. Conversely, we might anticipate that the decor of the missing handle of the Ilam Pan corresponded broadly to that of its bowl, both in its design and the range of its coloured enamel inlay. Indeed, the roundel motif would have been rather well-adapted to the available field, as on the Bad Pyrmont handle which has a frieze of four roundels (Henry 1933, fig. 32, 1).

Figure 5.10. The Bath Pan

The style and manufacture of the bowl of the Rudge Cup and Amiens Patera, if not their precise size, are closely linked, as also, though to a lesser extent, is that of the Hildburgh vessel, but the bowl of the Ilam Pan is distinctively different – it has an engraved, rather than relief-cast, inscription, lacks the 'mural' motif and differs in the nature of its enamelling. Nevertheless, its inscription relates it securely to the Rudge-type pans and it also shares with them the use of the blind A, which, although a common enough occurrence in inscriptions of this period, might yet imply a manufacturing link. The Rudge and Amiens pans would appear to have been purpose-made 'off-the-peg' inscribed Hadrian's Wall souvenirs. However, the Ilam vessel was probably manufactured purely as an exuberantly decorative pan which was subsequently customised as a souvenir of the Wall by the addition of a unique personalised inscription engraved in the available space below the rim. Perhaps this was a field reserved for such an addition, for it was used as such on the Rudge, Amiens and Beadlam pans as, too, on the splendid openwork silver frame of a blue glass *kantharos* from a third-century grave in the Varpelev cemetery near Himlingøje, Denmark (Grane 2007, 181, fig. 70). More broadly, it also references the position and nature of the inscription on the slightly earlier series of mould-blown glass 'circus beakers' (Allen 1998, 25-6). It is probably significant that the turquoise enamel inlay in the lettering of the Ilam Pan appears to be a shade different in colour to that in its decorative frieze, suggesting that they may not have been applied at the same time.

What was the purpose of the Ilam Pan other than as a souvenir of Hadrian's Wall? The series to which it belongs was a diminutive enamelled version of the common bronze deep-bowled handled pan. Since, in its plain form, that was the 'standard issue' legionary mess-tin, the form of the Rudge-type pans could be seen as singularly appropriate to a 'souvenir market' aimed at the military. Other deep-bowled pans, however, were more elaborate, including those made of silver which often incorporate religious iconography or bear votive inscriptions on their handle, as for example the pans from Backworth and Capheaton (Henig 1984, figs. 8, 11 and 48). More overtly religious and much closer in size to the enamelled pans is the silver pan from the Bath spring. A *punctim* inscription on the handle confirms that it was cast into the spring as a gift to Sulis (Brown 1988, 15-16, no. 24 and pl. XI; *RIB* II. 2, 2414.33), but heavy wear and substantial repairs to bowl and handle are suggestive of long usage prior to that. One of eight small handled pans, it was found deep in the ritual deposit on the southern side of the spring in the scree of material in front of the large arched window. With it was the Rudge variant bronze pan, with a punched dedication to Sulis Minerva on its handle, and a further six pewter pans of the same form, four of which were also inscribed to the goddess (Brown 1988, 14-20, nos. 23-5 and 28-32; Tomlin 1988). Cunliffe, observing that a number of the inscribed pans 'were well used after inscription', suggested that they may have been temple plate associated with official rituals rather than personal interventions and that their deposition may have occurred when they were no longer serviceable or as the result of a special ceremony (Cunliffe 1988, 361). A similarly long usage appears to be indicated by the wear and damage seen on some of the enamelled pans: those from Ilam, Rudge and Winterton lack their handle and base while the Scole and Ardownie handles display evidence of soldered and riveted repairs (Rogerson 1977, 142; Hunter 2006) and the Brougham pan, a Group C variant, has a riveted repair patch on the bowl, a probable replaced or repaired (riveted) base and a simple, plain, quite crude replacement handle (Cool 2004, 124-8, figs. 4.97 and 8.19).

It may be that the pans from the Bath spring were selected as votives purely because they had a role in the rituals and ceremonies performed in the sacred precinct but it is possible, too, that they were considered to be a particularly appropriate form of gift to the spring deity through their connection to water: in addition to the pouring of libations and serving of wine they may have been used as dipping pans to take water from the spring for ritual cleansing or as curative draughts, perhaps even to be drunk direct from the pans (Jackson 1990, 11-13; 1999, 115-6). Certainly, *contra* Cowen (Cowen and Richmond 1935, 311-2), who discounted use of the Rudge Cup as a drinking vessel on the strength of a perceived small capacity, the small handled pans could have held an appropriate quantity for drinking – about 160ml, a standard wine glass. Deep-bowled handled pans from other temple-spa sites, also suggestive of use with water in a ritual or curative context, include two from Baden with votive inscriptions to Mercury and one from Augst dedicated to Apollo and Sirona (Jackson 1990, 12).

More specifically, the spring context of the Bath Pan is shared by the Group C complete pan from Bad Pyrmont, a high-status ritual offering found in the Brodelbrunnen assemblage at the Roman-period thermal spring site east of the Teutoburger Wald in Free Germany (Müller 2002, 83-7). Significantly, too, the pans from Rudge and Amiens also have a watery or ritual context: Rudge from a well, Amiens from what may have been a household shrine associated with baths – the pan, which contained four bronze rings and seven studs, was found with a pipeclay mother goddess figurine in a room adjacent to a hypocausted chamber and small bath (Vasselle 1949/50, 230-3). To these can be added the Maltbæk pan, from a Danish bog deposit; the West Lothian Pan, which probably owes its remarkable state of preservation to deposition in water; and the London altar plaque from the River Thames. Thus, it is conceivable that the find-spot of the Ilam Pan, overlooking the rather remarkable River Manifold, may have been the location for ritual activity associated with the river and one or more deities. If the deposition of the Ilam Pan was, indeed, a ritual act in some way associated with water, then it involved a non-functioning vessel, either because it was a revered object, already old and damaged, or perhaps because it was deliberately de-functionalised by detaching the handle and base and delivering two heavy blows to the bowl. The most convenient and commonest field for the addition of a votive inscription to handled pans was the plain, flat underside of the handle: it is tantalising to think that the Ilam handle may have been inscribed, detached and separately dedicated.

Chapter 6
The Hildburgh Fragment

Lindsay Allason-Jones

The so-called Hildburgh Fragment is currently housed in the Victoria and Albert Museum, London. It is recorded as having been purchased in Barcelona in the early years of the twentieth century by Dr W. L. Hildburgh, who first loaned it to the Museum in 1920 (Loan Number 202). He briefly reclaimed it in 1935, possibly to allow John Cowen and/or Ian Richmond to study it for their paper in *Archaeologia Aeliana*; they record that it was on display in the Loan Court of the Victoria and Albert Museum (Cowen and Richmond 1935, 322, n. 23). Dr Hildburgh donated the Fragment to the Victoria and Albert Museum in 1949, when it was given the accession number M.78-1949. It was on display in the Museum between 1990 and 1999, but seems to have avoided the eye of Roman scholars during that time.

Figure 6.1. The exterior of the Hildburgh Fragment showing the 'inscription' (top right). Photo © Victoria and Albert Museum, London

Figure 6.2. The interior of the Hildburgh Fragment with the accession label visible.
Photo © Victoria and Albert Museum, London

The Fragment consists of the lower portion of a vessel and probably represents one third of its original circumference. The diameter of the roughly finished base is 60mm. There is no foot ring, suggesting that a wider base plate was applied externally. The greatest height surviving is 70mm. The piece has suffered damage in a number of ways: first, there are indications that it has been hit in several places by a pointed implement; two of the edges appear to have been deliberately cut, possibly in post-Roman times to tidy it up for sale or display; and the whole piece has been hammered to flatten it down, although not completely flat.

The piece has been decorated with champlevé enamelling with incised lines around the inner edges of the cast fields, presumably to provide firmer keying for the enamel. Little of the enamel survives, as was noted by Bateson (1981, 51) but through a microscope enough is discernible to confirm that the colours for each register were not, as suggested by Bateson, yellow and green, but turquoise, royal blue and red.

The lowest register is a series of downward pointing triangles, all with traces of turquoise enamel. The second register is a series of curling scrolls, all of which contained royal blue enamel. The third register consists of three rows of rectangles, arranged one above the other, all with turquoise enamel. The fourth register consists of a series of alternating rectangular panels within a continuous, crenellated border filled with red enamel, as also appears on the Rudge Cup, the Bath Pan and the Amiens Skillet. One panel type has four-petal motifs in reserved metal with turquoise enamel within the petals and in the surrounding fields, the other has a motif which contains two downward pointing pelta motifs surmounted by four rectangles arranged two above two; the upper edge has a series of three projecting wedges. Above this final register there is a plain area which contains some deliberately incised curved lines. These are not decorative nor do they represent cursive script; it is possible that they indicate a post-Roman owner's mark. There is no indication that the Fragment was inscribed with fort names.

Figure 6.3. Miss Noble's drawing of the Hildburgh Fragment as it appeared in *Archaeologia Aeliana*[4] 12 (1935) 323

There are a number of differences between the Fragment and the other vessels discussed in this volume (see Table 1.1). It has more registers of decoration than the others as well as one more row of small rectangles in its third register than the Rudge Cup. Where the Rudge Cup has panels of open squares with opposed peltae decoration, the Fragment has squares with four-petal motifs. Also, where the projections (crenellations) from the top of the 'turrets' on the Rudge Cup are shallow and straight-sided, those on the Fragment are wedge-shaped and noticeably larger and more akin to the motifs on the Bath Pan. The projections on the Bath Pan protrude from the panels with the four-petalled motifs, not the 'turrets', which on the Bath vessel are unconfined by the running red line and are 'upside down', with the two peltae above four rectangles (Figure 1.5). The Fragment does, however, have a lower range of elongated triangles, as can be seen on the vessels from Braughing, Maltbœk and West Lothian, although these three vessels each have a central band of stylised foliage with a laurel band above (Henry 1933, fig. 25. 2, 4, 6 respectively) (Figures 5.8 and 9.1).

Unlike the Rudge Cup and the Bath Pan there are no nicks around the motifs; instead the fields have been augmented by a sharply cut line around their edges. This different approach to ensuring that the enamel decoration is held firmly in the fields suggests these vessels were not made by the same craftsman. However, the limited range of decorative motifs suggests that the vessels may have been made in the same workshop or milieu or that the individual craftsmen had access to the same pattern book.

The inner surface is rough, as it would have emerged from the mould. In one area there is a clear ridge running up the piece which indicates a crack in the original clay mould. The size of the Fragment, the lack of any indication of a rim and the roughness of the interior suggest that this was not the base of a cup or *patera* but a larger vessel, the interior of which was not intended to be seen. This latter observation precludes the Fragment coming from a vase, such as the Beneventum Vase (Henry 1933, fig.23.1), a straight-sided vessel which has bands of enamelled motifs none of which replicate the motifs on the Fragment and associated vessels. Nor does the arrangement of the Fragment's enamelled decoration make its identification as part of a Castleford type flask likely (Bayley and Budd 1998). A more probable vessel form is that of a Catterick type flask, albeit of a larger size (Allason-Jones 2002), that is a vessel which bellies out from a narrow base before narrowing to a flared neck (Figure 9.4). A possible comparison can be made to a two-handled jug of unknown provenance published by Henry (1933, fig. 24. 4) even though this example does not share any decorative motifs with the Fragment.

Chapter 7

The Inscriptions on the Vessels

Paul Holder

The discovery in 2003 of the Ilam Pan has brought to three the number of inscribed 'Hadrian's Wall souvenirs'. There are significant differences between the form and contents of the inscription on this bowl and the other two. It therefore seems worthwhile to look anew at these texts as part of a publication which discusses enamelled bronzes from Roman Britain and these souvenirs in detail. In order of discovery the texts are:

Rudge Cup: .A.MAIS ABALLAVA VXELODVM CAMBOGLANS
BANNA

Amiens Patera: MAIS ABALLAVA VXELODVNVM CAMBOGLA̤[NI]S
BANNA ESICA[Symbol]

Ilam Pan: RIGORE VALI AELI DRACONIS MAIS COGGABATA
VXELODVNVM CAMMOGIANNA

The similarities in the inscriptions and in their decoration would suggest that the Rudge Cup and the Amiens Patera are similar in date. While the Ilam Pan is clearly a 'Hadrian's Wall souvenir' there are obvious differences in its decoration and in its inscription. An idea of its date in relation to the others could be crucial in explaining these differences. When considering these two aspects to try to date these bowls there is the potential for circularity of argument.

Stylistically the Rudge Cup and Amiens Patera along with the Hildburgh Fragment and the Bath Pan have similar decoration and are generally accepted as being manufactured in the second century (Cowen and Richmond 1935, 317-333; Moore 1978; Künzl 2008). Even the similarity with decoration on strap- or belt-terminals with lettering in the same style as the lettering on the Rudge Cup and Amiens Patera does not help (*RIB* II. 3, 2429.13 South Shields: VTERE / FELIX; *RIB* II.3 2429.14 South Shields: VTER[e] / FELI[x]; *RIB* II. 3, 2429.15 Chester: VTER[e] / FELI[x]. The letters are moulded but impressed rather than raised). These, too, cannot be dated independently from the bowls (Cowen and Richmond 1935, 325-326; 331-332; see also Allason-Jones, this volume). The Ilam Pan has different decoration and an incised inscription, part of which is the phrase RIGORE VALI AELI DRACONIS. The dating of this bowl turns on whether AELI defines VALI or is the family name of Draco. This personal name belongs either to the owner or to the maker of the bowl. If he had been the owner it has been suggested that he would have been awarded Roman citizenship either by Hadrian or by Antoninus Pius and that he would have been a retired auxiliary (Tomlin and Hassall 2004, 344 n. 47), though the lack of the *praenomen* Publius or Titus could indicate that Draco was descended from someone awarded citizenship by one of those emperors. The bowl could then be of third-century date, in which case Aelius Draco could well have been the maker rather than the owner. If he were the former he is more likely to have been descended from someone enfranchised by Hadrian or Antoninus Pius rather than having been awarded citizenship himself by either of the emperors. In the mid-second century a maker is more likely to have been a non-citizen.

The possibility of different names appearing on a list covering the same geographical route finds an exact parallel with the Vases Apollinaires found at Vicarello on Lake Bracciano in Italy (*CIL* XI 3281-3284). These four vases were deposited in a sacred spring and each has an inscription with the names of road stations between Cadiz and Rome. There are inconsistencies in spelling between the vases and vase 4 follows a different route through the Alpes Cottiae. It is thus believed that they were deposited at different dates within the reign of Augustus with vase 1 the earliest and vase 4 the latest (Rivet and Smith 1979, 35-36; in more detail, Heurgon 1952b, 172-175 especially 173).

The documentary sources for the names of the forts on Hadrian's Wall also show differences in which forts they include. The most complete list of what are now considered to be forts on Hadrian's Wall can be found in a document of early fifth century date (Rivet and Smith 1979, 216-218; Breeze 2006, 36). Fifteen forts appear in the section '*item per lineam valli*' of the command of the *Dux Britanniarum* in the *Notitia Dignitatum* in reverse order from that on the pans (*Not. Dig. Occ.* XL. 33 – XL. 48). Of these PONTE AELI, PETRIANIS, and CONCAVATA are named nowhere else in these forms. Comparison with the Ravenna Cosmography reveals apparent omissions in the *Notitia Dignitatum* because *Maia*, *Uxelodunum*, and *Banna* are lacking. In reality these can be restored to the Duke's list. PETRIANIS would appear to be a ghost name for *Uxelodunum*, where the *ala Petriana* was based, a scribe omitted *Banna* after *cohors I Aelia Dacorum*, and *Mais* became corrupted to MAGIS (Hassall 1976, 111-113; Mann 1989, 75 and 78; Holder 2004, 60-62). The *Ravenna Cosmography*, the other document, is an early eighth-century compilation of geographical names taken from earlier sources (Rivet and Smith 1979, 185-187; Breeze 2006, 39-40). The latest sources used in the British section seem to be of fourth-century date (Rivet and Smith 1979, 190-195). Here there is a group of 12 names which corresponds to those 'along the line of the wall' in the *Notitia Dignitatum*

Table 7.1. Hadrian's Wall fort names

Rudge Cup	Amiens Patera	Ilam Pan	Ravenna Cosmography	Notitia Dignitatum
MAIS	MAIS	MAIS	MAIA	–
–	–	COGGABATA	–	CONGAVATA
ABALLAVA	ABALLAVA	–	AVALANA	ABALLABA
VXELODVM	VXELODVNVM	VXELODVNVM	VXELLVDAMO	PETRIANIS
CAMBOGLANS	CAMBOGLA[..]S	CAMMOGIANNA	–	AMBOGLANNA
BANNA	BANNA	–	BANNA	–
–	–	–	–	MAGNIS
–	ESICA	–	ESICA	AESICA
–	–	–	–	VINDOLANA
–	–	–	VELVRTION	BORCOVICIO
–	–	–	BROCOLITI	PROCOLITIA
–	–	–	CELVNO	CILVRNO
–	–	–	ONNO	HVNNO
–	–	–	VINDOVALA	VINDOBALA
–	–	–	CONDECOR	CONDERCO
–	–	–	–	PONTE AELI
–	–	–	SERDVNO	SEGEDVNO

also in reverse order from that on the pans (*Ravenna Cosmography* (Schnetz 1942) 107.24-107.29). Among stations on a route between LAGVBALVMI (Carlisle) and VINOVIA (Binchester) are MAGNIS and VINDOLANDE with GABAGLANDA in between (*Ravenna Cosmography* 107.10-107.13). Elsewhere there is a duplicate entry MAIO for *Maia* and, between Hadrian's Wall and the Antonine Wall, there appears CAMBROIANNA (*Ravenna Cosmography* 107.5; 107.36). This may well be an entry for *Camboglanna* which was missed from its correct location and added later (Dillemann 1979, 69; Rivet and Smith 1979, 293-294).

With the examples of different names and variant spellings in the documentary sources as well as the evidence from the Vases Apollinaires it is not surprising that there are discrepancies between the inscriptions on the bowls. This may well be evidence for the bowls being produced at different dates. A short review of the archaeological evidence for Hadrian's Wall forts westward from the Irthing Gorge where the Wall was originally built of turf is instructive. There is now sufficient evidence to show that all the forts added to the Turf Wall were originally built of turf and timber (Bidwell 1999, 21). These were Birdoswald, Stanwix, Drumburgh, and Bowness. Castlesteads was not attached to the Wall but the Vallum diverted around the site. It, too, was originally turf and timber (Bidwell 1999, 21). However, the fort attached to the Wall at Burgh-by-Sands was built across the line of the Turf Wall but with the later Stone Wall aligned on its northern corners (Burgh II: Breeze 2006, 350-353; Hodgson 2009, 153-154). The fort occupied in the reign of Hadrian was constructed of turf and timber and was situated 1km south-west (Burgh I: Breeze and Woolliscroft 2009, 59-74). Birdoswald, Castlesteads, Stanwix, and Bowness were re-occupied after the withdrawal from the Antonine Wall. However, there is no evidence for Drumburgh being re-occupied at this time. Rather the second fort, stone-built, was bonded with the later stone wall (Breeze 2006, 359-361). The stone fort at Stanwix was built after the Turf Wall had been replaced by stone (Breeze 2006, 341-345).

These identified and dated fort sites match the combined place names on the bowls:

> MAIS appears as a fort name on each of the bowls. The name form is a neuter plural and *Maia* is therefore likely to be the correct nominative as recorded in the *Ravenna Cosmography* (Rivet and Smith 1979, 408). As the westernmost fort on Hadrian's Wall it can be identified with Bowness-on-Solway.

> COGGABATA appears only on the Ilam Pan but seems to be the equivalent of the CONGAVATA of the *Notitia Dignitatum*. *Congabata* is the presumed correct form of the name (Tomlin and Hassall 2004, 344, fn. 47). This can be located at Drumburgh which is a small fort occupied under Hadrian which was not immediately re-occupied after the withdrawal from the Antonine Wall later in the second century.

> ABALLAVA is included on the Rudge Cup and the Amiens Patera but not on the Ilam Pan. This is the correct form of the fort name as confirmed by an inscription which mentions a *cuneus Frisionum Aballavensium* (*RIB* I 883; Rivet and Smith 1979, 238). This fort can be located in the village of Burgh-by-Sands where the fort on Hadrian's Wall was apparently built no earlier than when Hadrian's Wall was re-occupied following the withdrawal from the Antonine Wall (though see Breeze below p.108).

> VXELODVNVM is named on the Amiens Patera and Ilam Pan while the name VXELODVM appears on the Rudge Cup. The latter may be an abbreviation rather than an error (Rivet and Smith 1979, 31). *Uxelodunum* is the correct form of the name (Rivet and Smith 1979, 483). The position of this fort between *Aballava* and *Camboglanna* shows that it is to be located at Stanwix.

CAMBOGLA[NI]S can be restored on the Amiens Patera and it appears as CAMBOGLAN(i)S on the Rudge Cup. This appears as CAMMOGIANNA on the Ilam Pan as a result of copying errors (Tomlin and Hassall 2004, 344, fn. 47). The apparent correct form of the name is *Camboglanna* which is a neuter plural (Rivet and Smith 1979, 293). Unusually it is found in different cases at different dates (Rivet and Smith 1979, 33). The fort is located at Castlesteads.

BANNA appears on the Rudge Cup and Amiens Patera and this is the correct form of the place name (Rivet and Smith 1979, 261-262). It should be located at Birdoswald which is confirmed by an altar set up there by the *venatores Banniess(es)* (*RIB* I 1905).

ESICA is named only on the Amiens Patera. This form of the name is also found in the *Ravenna Cosmography* but the correct one, *Aesica*, is recorded in the *Notitia Dignitatum* (Rivet and Smith 1979, 242). This should be located at the next fort eastward along the curtain of Hadrian's Wall from Birdoswald which is Great Chesters (Carvoran is between Birdoswald and Great Chesters but is not on Hadrian's Wall and is even outside the Vallum).

CONCLUSIONS

Commentators on the Rudge Cup and the Amiens Patera have suggested that each was part of a set (Cowen and Richmond 1935, 332 and 341-342; Heurgon 1951, 24; Rivet and Smith 1979, 233). The other bowls would have been inscribed with the names of the other forts on Hadrian's Wall. However, the question of which place-names may have been inscribed on the extra bowls has hardly been addressed. The newly discovered Ilam Pan has an inscription with a list of names which again covers only the western end of Hadrian's Wall. But it also includes a descriptive phrase which potentially weakens this thesis. It is unclear whether other bowls in a potential set would also have been inscribed with the phrase *rigore vali Aeli Draconis*. If they were not, how would it be known they were part of a set? If they were, it would affect how many items would have been in such a set.

Two more bowls, for example, would have been needed for a set comprising bowls of the same size as either the Rudge Cup or the Amiens Patera. The inscription on the former has 36 letters. If it is accepted that the 12 place names at the beginning of the third British section of the *Ravenna Cosmography* would be the Hadrian's Wall forts recorded on such bowls then an estimate of the length of further inscriptions can be made. The fort names from *Aesica* to *Segedunum* would comprise about 66 letters. These could be accommodated neatly on two more bowls of the same size. On the other hand, the text on the Amiens Patera included an extra name and occupied 43 letters. The remaining fort names in its set would have been from *Vercovicium* to *Segedunum* and would have required about 61 letters. These would not fit on two bowls of the same size without the blank areas being filled with some sort of decoration perhaps like the zig-zag pattern on the Beadlam Pan. An alternative would be to argue for bowls of different sizes in a set; in which case the 'Amiens' set would have needed only a second item if it had been the same size as the Hildburgh Fragment or Beadlam Pan. These inconsistencies in visualising a set with Hadrian's Wall fort names suggest it is more likely that these souvenirs were single items.

It would seem that the Ilam Pan is the earliest of these souvenirs and was made by Draco. It can be dated to late in the reign of Hadrian at a time when it would seem that Hadrian's Wall was known as the *Vallum Aelium* (Tomlin and Hassall 2004, 344, fn. 47). Later, when *Aballava* was located on Hadrian's Wall and *Congabata* was unoccupied, the Rudge Cup and Amiens Patera were made. This was in the second century after the death of Antoninus Pius. The balance of evidence suggests each bowl was a single item rather than part of a set. The discovery of moulds for enamelled flasks at Castleford in the early second century demonstrates that manufacturers could be based close to military installations. If the choice of names of forts at the western end of Hadrian's Wall has particular significance it could be because there was a large population at Carlisle among whom must have been bronze workers (see also Henig 2010/11, 13).

Chapter 8

Enamelled vessels and related objects reported to the Portable Antiquities Scheme 1997-2010

Sally Worrell

INTRODUCTION

This report compiles the enamelled copper alloy vessels and related objects that have so far been recorded by the Portable Antiquities Scheme (PAS). The PAS was founded in 1997 and was extended to cover the whole of England and Wales during 2003. In each area Finds Liaison Officers record finds reported by members of the public on an online database (www.finds.org.uk). By March 2012 775,000 artefacts had been recorded. The database is publicly accessible and searchable. Database identifiers for the objects published here are provided below which will allow interested readers to access further images. Where these objects have been published in the annual roundup of Roman period finds reported to the scheme in the journal *Britannia* (since 2004) this is indicated below.

The most commonly occurring object is the handled pan, but where, as in most cases, only a terminal fragment survives it is difficult if not impossible to distinguish between shallow and deep-handled pans and handled strainers. Jars and other vessels including containers in the form of cockerels, bath flasks (specifically the swivels for their suspension), pyxides and a candlestick are also included.

PANS

Winterton, Lincolnshire (PAS number: NLM-F50443).
Found by Mr Hancock. Recorded by L. Staves and S. Worrell. Acquired by North Lincolnshire Museum (Worrell 2009, 294, no. 12, colour fig. 5)

An incomplete copper-alloy pan in polychrome champlevé enamel (Figure 8.1). The body of the pan is convex and on one side has sustained some damage. The rim is pushed in, no trace of a handle now survives and the base is missing. The body is decorated with an enamelled chequerboard pattern of four rows and 33 columns of square cells. Although the enamel does not survive in all cells, it is clear that each row and column has alternating red, dark blue, turquoise/pale blue and yellow squares. Diagonal lines of same-coloured cells recur, but there are insufficient columns for this pattern to be fully repeated. Much of the light green patina has worn off inside the bowl and on the exterior of the rim. The bowl is 38mm high, its distorted external rim varies between 51.5mm and 92.5mm in diameter, the thickness of the rim is 1.8-2.6mm and the base diameter is 58mm. The vessel weighs 112.6g.

Figure 8.1. The Winterton Pan

The form of the Winterton pan and colour used on it are very similar to the Ilam Pan (Worrell 2004, 325, no. 8, frontispiece; Jackson, this volume). Based largely on the style of ornament, enamelled pans have been classified into three main groups, as well as a group which does not fit within the classification (Moore 1978, 325-6, no. 1, D.1, fig. 2.1). The Winterton Pan fits into this unclassified group and is very similar in form and decorative style to a pan with a bi-chrome chequerboard pattern of blue on white enamel from Bingen, near Mainz, Germany (Moore 1978, 326, no. D.1; Henry 1933, ii, 116, fig. 28, 2). A chequerboard pattern of square cells with red, blue and green enamel is also found on the Rudge Cup, representing Hadrian's Wall, and in blue, red, green and yellow enamel on a container in the form of a cockerel from Cologne (Moore 1978, no. 1, fig. 2.1; Menzel 1986, 59, no. 122, Taf. 78).

Reepham, Norfolk (PAS number: NMS-47B176)
Found by P. Buckley. Recorded by S. Ashley.
The trapezoidal terminal of a pan handle fragment which carries cast symmetrical foliate decoration, with paired leaves springing from a central

stem, two in the form of pointed ovals and two with curling tendrils, on an orange enamelled field (Figure 8.2). A narrow band of pale blue enamel survives in places close to the damaged outer edges. The object is 30mm long and 28mm wide.

Attleborough, Norfolk (PAS number: NMS 1518)
Found by D. Howlett. Recorded by S. Ashley.

The broken terminal of a pan handle, trapezoidal in shape with an appliqué plate broken at the short end (Figure 8.3). It carries elaborate symmetrical cast foliate decoration on a blue enamelled field. Other edges are damaged. The fragment measures at least 30mm by 45mm.

Southease, East Sussex (PAS number: SUR-4DE0E1)
Identified by D. Williams.

A very worn fragment, possibly from a *patera* handle. The flat handle has indistinct decoration which was probably inlaid with enamel and also has incised and crossed decoration. The object is 41mm long and weighs 12.9g.

Figure 8.2. The Reepham Pan handle

Figure 8.3. The Attleborough Pan handle

Gunthorpe, Norfolk (PAS number: NMS-7BC635)
Found by T. Hudson. Recorded by A. Rogerson. Note added by J. Pearce.

An enamelled trilobed terminal of a pan handle at the centre of which in a triangular field are the words *bebe sese* (Tomlin 2011, 450, 15, fig. 13) (Figure 8.4). The letters have been filled with red enamel, although in places the engraving is so shallow and narrow that no enamel survives. Both words are followed by a small triangular enamel-filled cell. Above and below the inscription, following the sides of the handle is a running scroll reserved against a (now empty) enamelled field. The object has a maximum width of 36mm, a minimum width of 24mm and its surviving length is 35mm.

Figure 8.4. The Gunthorpe Pan handle

The Inscription
John Pearce

The most plausible interpretation of *bebe sese* may be as a paired motto, 'drink' and 'live long', if *sese* is correctly read as a variant form of *zeses*. The variant *bebe* for *bibe* is not yet otherwise attested in Britain, though it is occasionally documented elsewhere. No parallel has yet been found for the variant form *sese*, either in Britain or elsewhere. Though the exhortations 'bibe' and 'zeses', the latter both in Latin transliteration and in Greek, are commonly documented, especially on glass and Rhenish colour coat drinking vessels, their pairing on the same vessel is not attested (*Zeses*: Glass vessels: *RIB* II. 2, 2419.72 (Canterbury); *RIB* II. 2, 2419.43 (Exeter); *RIB* II. 2, 2419.45 (Wint Hill); *RIB* II.2, 2419.46 (Caerwent); also on two gold rings *RIB* II. 3, 2422.1, 2422.10. *Bibe*: several examples at *RIB* II. 6, 2498). The closest parallels to its spirit occur on the handful of vessels whose mottoes combine an encouragement to drink (*bibere*) and live (*vivere*), most famously perhaps the so-called 'Trivulzio' cage cup, *Bibe vivas multis annis*. (*CIL Supplementa Italica*, 1083.2). The occurrence of a text of this type on this vessel form is unusual: makers' stamps predominate among the texts documented on handled pans, the handful of exceptions being marks of ownership or dedications to gods (e.g. *RIB* II. 2, 2414.36, a dedication to the Matres on a silver pan handle from Backworth; *RIB* II. 2, 2415.60, a dedication to Sulis at Bath). (Figure 1.5)

OTHER VESSELS

Colkirk, Norfolk (PAS number: NMS1109)
Found by N. Abram. Recorded by S. Ashley.

An irregular fragment of a copper-alloy vessel, possibly from the side of a bowl, bearing a scale pattern with recessed cells of blue enamel and a band of running scroll on a red enamelled field. The fragment has dimensions of 23 by 29mm.

Feltwell, Norfolk (PAS number: NMS-FFBFB1)
Found by D. Woollestone. Recorded by A. Rogerson.

Figure 8.5. The pedestal base found at Feltwell

An incomplete pedestal base from a copper alloy flask (Figure 8.5). At the base it is decorated externally with a row of extended triangular cells in green, red and blue enamel but with no detectable sequence. The fragment has an external diameter of 29mm and is 28mm high. Similar vessels with a pedestal base are known, including a two-handled vase from Ambleteuse, Pas-de-Calais (Kaufmann-Heinimann 1998, 235, GF13, Abb. 186). Jars without handles include a small, pear-shaped flask tapering to a narrow disc base with two rows of enamelled elongated triangles and crescents arranged in four registers in red and blue enamel on the body from Catterick, North Yorkshire (Allason-Jones 2002, 78-80, no. 1, fig. 268) (Figure 9.4). Other similar flasks include an example from Gladbach, Germany and from an uncertain provenance in the Fitzwilliam Museum, Cambridge (Lindenschmidt 1864-1911, pl. 4, no. 7; Henry 1933, 135, fig. 43.3).

Sutton, Suffolk (PAS number: SF10415)
Found by P. Hammond. Identified by R. Jackson. Recorded by F. Minter.

An almost complete copper-alloy panel deriving from a small hexagonal

Figure 8.6. The Sutton vase

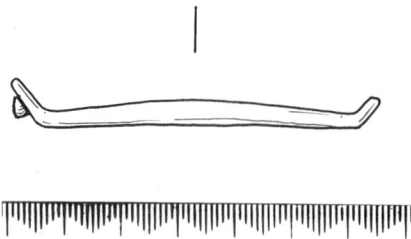

Figure 8.7. The Sutton vase

vase, which tapers from top to bottom (Figures 8.6 and 8.7). The panel is rectangular but flares out towards the terminal end, measuring 43mm long and 32mm wide at its broadest point. It has raised flanges protruding from both of the long edges of the front face at an angle of about 45°; these flanges are 3mm in height and run for the entire length of the panel. At 13mm from the wider end of the panel the flanges had rivets on their back face; one rivet survives. The separate panels of the vase body were rivetted together by these flanges. The front face of the panel is decorated with an incised pattern inlaid with blue enamel of a central oval-shape with pairs of scrolled spirals above, below and within it. The back face is flat and undecorated. There is a near-complete vase of similar type (of unknown provenance) in the Rheinisches Landesmuseum, Bonn, and panel fragments include one from Silchester, Hants. (R. Jackson *pers. comm.*, 2003).

Perlthorpe cum Budby, Nottinghamshire (PAS number: DENO-54B3D1)
Found by J. Kirk. Identified by K. Leahy and recorded by R. Atherton.
(Worrell 2006, 441-442, no. 9, fig. 10)

An enamelled copper-alloy swivel from an oil flask (Figures 8.8 and 8.9). The body is rectangular with a longitudinal central cylindrical perforation. There is a circular collar around the perforation at the base of the object, and projecting from each top corner of the body is a hook ending in a rounded

Figure 8.8. The swivel found at Perlthorpe cum Budby

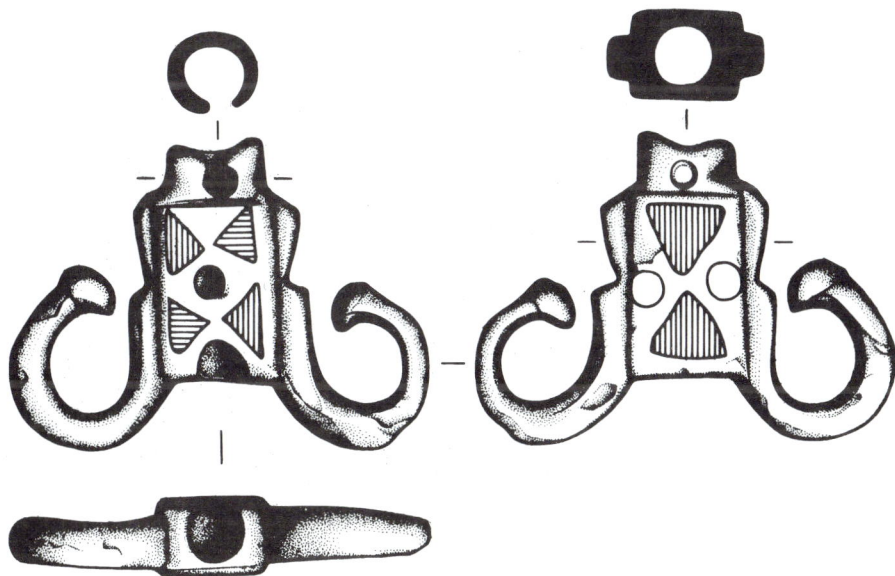

Figure 8.9. The swivel found at Perlthorpe cum Budby

knop, which would have held a pair of chains for the suspension of the flask (cf. Liversidge 1968, 137, fig. 50). Both faces of the rectangular body are decorated with champlevé enamel cells; one face with two opposing triangles of red enamel with a circle of green enamel to either side, the other with two rows of opposing red, blue and possibly green enamel cells. There are three rivet holes on one face; one at the top, one in the middle of the body, and one through the base of the collar but there do not appear to be any rivet holes on the other face. Neither of the two loops has signs of obvious wear, although there is some damage to the outer surfaces of the loops. The swivel is 26.57mm long, 37.35mm wide from loop to loop, 7.7mm thick and it weighs 12.85g. A similar example with a double hook and applied decoration on both sides of the centre-piece, but also with a suspension loop passing through a hole at the top is known from Woodstock, Oxon. (Kirk 1949, 27, no. H.3, pl. III B).

Ludham, Norfolk (PAS number: NMS-07F828)
Found by S. W. Merralls. Recorded by A. Rogerson.

A round socketed knob, probably from a vessel lid (Figure 8.10). The round socket narrows from the flaring base and has a patch of white material, probably fixative on its flat end. The exterior is offset before expanding to an overhanging rim around the upper surface, on which there is in the centre a round projection with concave top and a round rib around the edge. The two fields between the rim and rib, and rib and central projection, may have been inlaid with enamel, but now contain small areas of green and grey corrosion products. The underside of the rim is decorated with a broad tongue-and-dart moulding. The object is 31mm high, its top diameter is 39mm, the base diameter is 37mm, the depth of the socket is 25mm and it weighs 64.8g. No good parallel has been found.

Figure 8.10. The knob found at Ludham

Reigate, Surrey (PAS number: SUR-9891E5)
Found by R. Mintey. Recorded by D. Williams.

A circular shallow flat-topped dome (Figure 8.11). Around the circumference is a series of 15 recessed triangles; there are no traces of enamel within them. Projecting from the centre is a rivet which is also visible within the concave reverse. The object has a diameter of 34mm, is 9mm thick and weight 9.94g. The object is perhaps the base of a composite vessel such as a candle holder. A possibly analogous object may be the base of a candlestick in the Fitzwilliam Museum, Cambridge from an unknown provenance in Britain which carries various motifs including enamelled rectangles, elongated triangles and rows of leaves (Henry 1933, 114, fig. 27.1).

Figure 8.11. The dome found at Reigate

Thonock, Lincolnshire (PAS number: LIN-D6E2B1)
Found by J. and L. Bennett. Identified by M. Henig and E. Künzl, recorded by S. Worrell and A. Daubney. (E. Künzl *pers. comm.*; Worrell 2009, 295-297, no. 13, colour fig. 6 and fig. 7).

An incomplete three-dimensional copper-alloy enamelled fish, of uncertain function, perhaps a vessel attachment or lock bolt and dating to the early second century (Figures 8.12 and 8.13). The hollow fish comprises two joining halves, one of which is heavily damaged. Traces of what appears to be solder survive on the internal surfaces of each half at head and tail. On each side is a triangular lateral fin and on one side a small, triangular dorsal fin, decorated with finely incised lines, survives. The base is flat and the tail is mostly missing on one side. On the other it curves strongly upwards, terminating in a rounded end, although the tail fin is missing. Situated beneath the fish's gill, the base has a rectangular fitting (12mm long, 9mm wide, 1.5mm thick) which projects from the right side. There are mouldings but no sign of a similar projection on the left side. On both sides the eyes are represented by a dot of blue enamel surrounded by a ring of black enamel. The gills and mouth are also picked out in black enamel and the body and tail are decorated with up to four rows of crescent (half moon) cells at the widest part of the fish, filled with green enamel. The fish is 67mm long and 12mm wide at its widest point. The two halves weigh 10.1g and 9.5g.

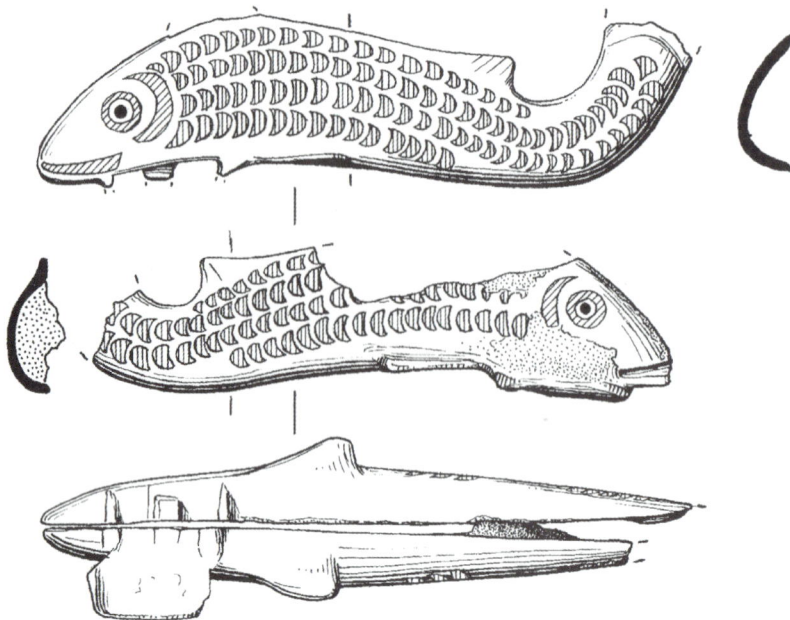

Figure 8.12. The fish found at Thonock

Figure 8.13. The fish found at Thonock

Direct parallels for this object have not yet been identified, although its decoration resembles that on Romano-British enamelled vessels of Künzl's neo-Celtic style group, as seen for example on the flask with crescent and elongated triangle cells in red and blue enamel from Catterick (Künzl 1995, 39-50; Allason-Jones 2002, 78-80, fig. 268, pl. 96) (Figure 9.4).

ENAMELLED COCKERELS

Cople, Bedfordshire (PAS number: SOM-745EA2)
Found by C. Giddings. Recorded by L. Burnett, S. Worrell and J. Pearce (Worrell and Pearce 2011, 419-421, online figs. 5-6, fig. 17). (Drawing by M. Trevarthen)

Figure 8.14. The cockerel found at Cople

An enamelled copper-alloy container in the form of a cockerel standing on a pedestal, now in two fragments (Figures 8.14 to 8.16). The cockerel is 68.4mm high, excluding the legs, 106.7mm, including the legs and base, c.72mm beak to tail and has a maximum width of 43.3mm across the chest: the two pieces together weigh 105g. The head, comb, neck, half of the body and legs are present, but the tail, wings, back, wattle and lower beak are missing. The cockerel is hollow with an opening from neck to tail which would have been covered by the back and wings. The missing tail and wattle would have been cast separately.

Figure 8.15. The cockerel found at Cople

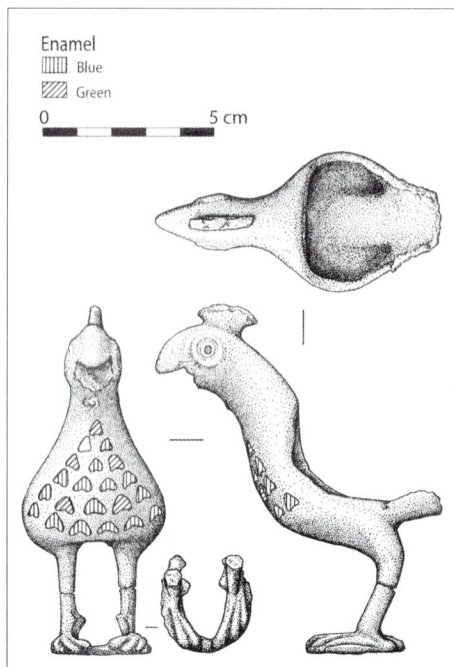

Enamel
▦ Blue
▨ Green
0   5 cm

Figure 8.16. The cockerel found at Cople

The eyes are formed by raised discs in reserved metal, with an indented central dot of blue enamel surrounded by an incised circle. The comb is directly over the eye and two indents in its curved upper edge divide it into three sections. A rough point on the underside of the head indicates where the wattle was attached.

The chest is decorated with six rows of triangular and arched cells which represent stylised plumage. These are inlaid in a stepped arrangement and with each row decrease in number by one cell from six at the base to one at the apex. The top cell is green, in the second row one cell is missing, the other is blue, in the third and fifth rows blue and green cells alternate, and in the fourth and sixth all cells are blue. In the sixth row all cells are curved.

On the lower legs small spurs project inward and the three toes of each foot, which survive complete, curve and follow the contour of the horse-shoe shaped flat pedestal. The survival of the lower legs, feet and pedestal is unusual as in most cases the body and upper legs are broken and separated from the stand. The form of the Cople pedestal is not known on any other cockerels of this type from the north-west provinces. Birds from Ezinge, Groningen, Netherlands and Tongeren, Belgium, for example, both stand on a concave pedestal on a small domed base (Jitta, Peters and van Es 1967, 114 no. 47; De Schaetzen and Vanderhoeven 1956, 23; Faider-Feytmans 1979, 134, no. 238, pl. 97).

Slyne with Hest, Lancashire (PAS number: LANCUM-361F75).
Found by I. Sharp. Recorded by D. Boughton and S. Worrell. (Worrell 2006, 436-437, no. 3, fig. 4)

An enamelled copper-alloy container, now in three joining fragments which make up the head, neck and body of a cockerel (Figure 8.17). The cockerel is 123mm high, 101mm long and 52mm wide at the broadest part of the chest. The legs are broken off and the tail and wattle, which was cast separately and attached to the underside of the beak with a short lug, are missing (a surviving circular wattle may be seen attached to the underside of the beak on a very similar example from Tongeren: (Faider-Feytmans 1979, 134, no. 238 pl. 97)). The bird's detached back, which also served as a lid, is decorated with irregularly arranged square and near-square cells inlaid with red and blue enamel. The chest is decorated with rows of triangular and arched cells inlaid with blue, green and red enamel arranged in a pyramidal format. The second, fourth and sixth rows are in blue and the third and fifth have alternating red and green cells. The enamel in the uppermost row is missing. The eyes are represented by a central dot of blue enamel surrounded by a ring of red enamel. The cockerel's back and wings were cast separately and acted as a lid to the container, although there is no trace of a hinge or other fitting. Traces of the clay core from the mould still remain inside the head and neck.

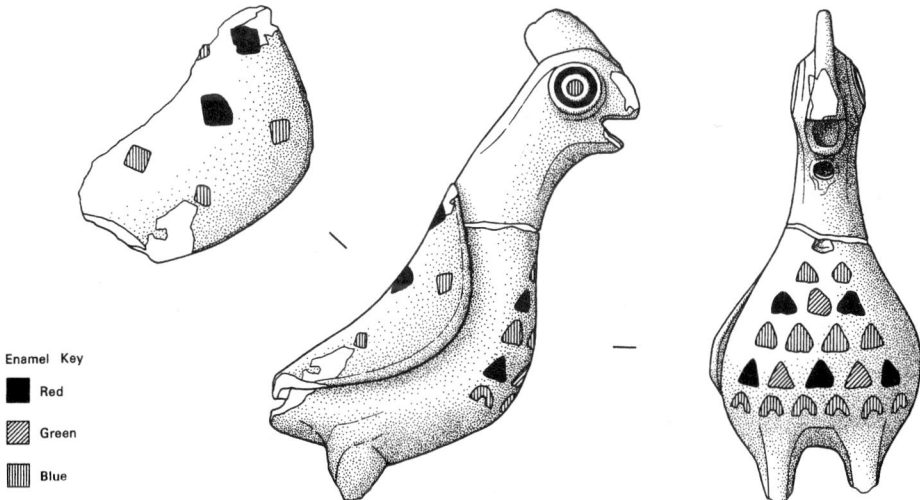

Enamel Key

Red

Green

Blue

Figure 8.17. The cockerel found at Slyne with Hest

Only a few such vessels, which probably date to the late second to early third centuries, are known from the north-western provinces. Similar examples to those from Cople and Slyne-with-Hest include instances from London (Anon. 1922, 94, fig. 116), Bridges Garage site, Cirencester,

Gloucestershire (E. R. McSloy *pers. comm.*), Cologne (Menzel 1986, 59, no. 122, Taf. 78), Tongeren (Faider-Feytmans 1979, 134, no. 238 pl. 97) and Cologne (this item was formerly at Worms museum: Henry 1933, 138, fig. 43.1; see Figure 2.7 above). The cockerels from Tongeren and Slyne-with-Hest are remarkably similar, both in their size and their enamelled decoration, consisting of triangular and crescentic cells on the underside of the body: they are possibly products of the same workshop. Centres of Roman provincial bronze and enamel working at that time were the Rhineland and Belgium, from which enamelled bronzes were traded to more distant parts of the Empire, for example Pannonia, as well as Britain (Exner 1939, 88, Henry 1933 139-141).

The most commonly accepted interpretation of the function of these objects is as oil lamps (De Schaetzen and Vanderhoeven, 1956, 23; Faider-Feytmans, 1979, 134-141, no. 238). However, while this may be possible for the cockerels from Tongeren and Slyne-with-Hest, Menzel (1986, 60) argued that it may not have been for those from Cologne and London due to their shape and the fact that the lids (wings) were soldered to the bodies of the birds, making it difficult to refill them. In at least one case, from Buchten, Netherlands, an alternative votive use is attested. The cockerel's feet rest on an angled disk attached to the pedestal below, which carries an incised inscription dedicating the object by a veteran of the Sixth Legion, Ulpius Verinus, to the goddess Arcanua, a deity only otherwise attested on a single stone inscription from the same place (*AE* 1983, 723: *Deae Arcanu(a)e Ulpius Verinus veteranus leg(ionis) VI v(otum) s(olvit) l(ibens) m(erito)*; cf. *AE* 1983, 724, Vermeulen-Bekkering n.d.)

Chapter 9

Frontier finds, frontier art – views of enamelled vessels

Fraser Hunter

INTRODUCTION

The enamelled pan from West Lothian is among the finest enamelled vessels from Britain, and the writer was asked to contribute a note on it for the sake of completeness of this volume. This revitalised a string of intermittent investigations over the years which, while casting frustratingly little light on the object itself, have led down a number of interesting byways. This contribution is the result: starting from the two known Scottish finds, issues of typology and decoration will be touched upon before dwelling in more detail on the category of vessels which Künzl has termed 'neo-Celtic', since this is particularly relevant to the development of art on the British frontier. A final section will consider finds from beyond the frontier, while an Appendix lists recent and unnoted British finds as a supplement to the listings of Moore (1978), Künzl (1995), and Worrell's treatment of the PAS finds (this volume).

THE ENAMELLED PAN FROM WEST LOTHIAN
(with scientific analysis by Susy Kirk)

On 10 April 1865, John Nicholson of Kirkcudbright exhibited a 'Small Pot or Patella of yellow-coloured Bronze ... covered with enamel, arranged in ornamental scrolls, leaves &c.' to the Society of Antiquaries of Scotland in Edinburgh (*Proc. Soc. Antiq. Scot.* 6, (1864-6) 183). After this first appearance in the academic literature, the object vanished until 1884, when it was purchased by the Society. It was then promptly and fully published by Joseph Anderson, along with known comparanda, and has been oft-quoted ever since (e.g. Anderson 1885; Curle 1932, 302-6; Toynbee 1962, 174, cat. 113; Moore 1978, 325-6, B1). It is now in the collections of the National Museum of Scotland (registration number FA 43). However, its discovery and subsequent history are shrouded in mystery.

It is unclear how John Nicholson acquired the item, although Trotter (1901, 23) recorded 'he possessed many antiquarian treasures, in particular a ring containing a miniature of Prince Charlie, presented by the Prince to

Figure 9.1. The West Lothian Pan; a, overall view; b, detail of bowl decoration;
c, variant decoration under handle; d, handle

Flora Macdonald, which his wife inherited'. Although the exhibition notice
records him as a bookseller, he had an altogether more chequered life than
this rather genteel description would indicate (Trotter 1901, 23, 41; Harper
1876, 65-6). Born in the parish of Tongland, just north of Kirkcudbright,
in 1778 (or 1777, according to Harper), he was apprenticed as a weaver,
subsequently moving to Glasgow to follow this trade. At a time of slack work
he joined the army and fought in the Napoleonic Wars, leaving the forces in
1814 to return to weaving. This proved a temporary shift, with the changing
industry leading him to abandon it and become a pedlar, selling books and
stationery. He returned to Kirkcudbright in 1820 to establish himself as a
bookseller and printer. He died on 11 September 1866, and it is unclear what
happened to the pan on his death. As is typical for the time, the Society's
archives do not record from whom the vessel was purchased; no relevant
correspondence has yet been located, and the Purchase Committee minutes
of 26 July 1884 record only that:

> It was agreed to authorise Dr Anderson to negotiate for the
> purchase of the enamelled patella of bronze found in Linlith-
> gowshire at or under £15.

It seems likely that it passed to his son, James, who 'inherits also the antiquarian leanings of his father' (Harper 1876, 66), and donated some objects to Kirkcudbright Museum after it was founded in 1879 (D. Devereux *pers. comm.*). This would suggest that information on the vessel was reliable, as it came from his father, but it cannot yet be demonstrated that James owned the vessel, or was responsible for selling it to the National Museum.

The object's excellent condition – it is unpatinated and almost undamaged, with the enamelling in remarkable condition – indicates it came from a bog or similar waterlogged context, but there are no clues to its findspot beyond the 'Linlithgowshire' of Anderson's 1885 account; the original exhibition note makes no mention of provenance, and we can only presume that Anderson had access to information at the time of acquisition which is now lost. Certainly there are no grounds to doubt Anderson's reliability, although one might have reservations over Nicholson's; his varied career included an episode of alleged plagiarism over a book which he published (J. Hunter 2008, 75-6). However, at present 'Linlithgowshire' is all we have to go on. Linlithgowshire and West Lothian are synonymous, although in recent times the former has fallen from use, and the modern political region does not follow the old county boundaries precisely.

One would think that some early source would mention the discovery of so striking an object, but this has so far been a vain hope: discoveries of Roman vessel handles alone are mentioned from Inchgarvie House and near Dundas Castle, Dalmeny, while 'a brass pot, and in it a pagan idol', found near Queensferry in 1738, were 'instantly demolished' (*Old Statistical Account* 1 (1792) 238; *New Statistical Account* 2 (1845), 103; RCAHMS 1929, 208-9; Robertson 1970, 221). The trail, at the moment, is cold. Roman sites are known in the shire; the eastern end of the Antonine Wall, a probable fort at Linlithgow, perhaps some station at Blackness, and fortlets at Castle Greg and Livingston (Keppie 2004, 126, 131-2). It is tempting to link the discovery to the Roman presence, but it could equally have come into indigenous hands, as discussed below; the deposition of Roman vessels in wet locations, probably as ritual deposits, was common to both (F. Hunter 1997, 117-8). The *New Statistical Account* (2 (1845) 36, 91, 150) refers to the draining of various mosses around the relevant period.

The vessel is made of three separate components, soldered together: the enamelled body, an enamelled handle and a plain base (Figure 9.2). Descriptions below orientate the vessel with the handle at 12 o'clock. The solder holding the handle to the body is uncorroded and plainly modern, although traces of a darker solder above and below suggest this is where it was originally fastened. The right-hand tip of the handle, where it fastens to the rim, is a later repair. The base is clearly a replacement, being of uncorroded, unpitted brass with filemarks. The lack of extensive abrasion indicates the vessel has not been cleaned upon discovery. The enamelling appears at first sight to be in excellent condition, although it has been 'improved', with gaps filled with wax. There are only minor fillings on the body, but the handle is extensively restored: the green is original, the blue partly original, but only a tiny fragment of the original red survives. There is enough, however, to indicate the restoration is accurate.

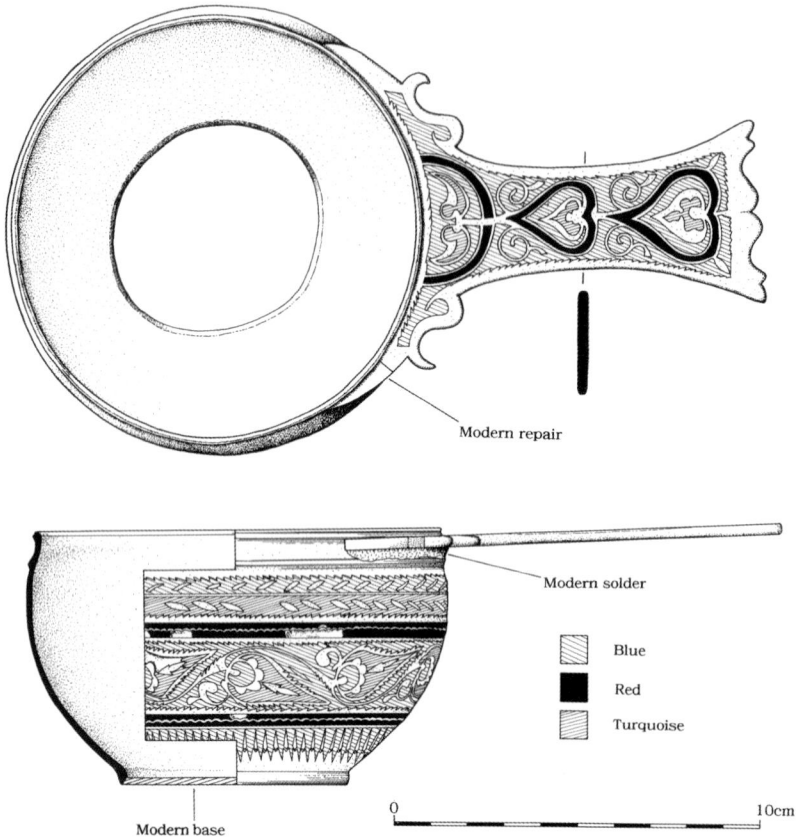

Figure 9.2. The West Lothian Pan: technical details

The pan has a shallow concave moulding below the rounded rim (Figure 9.2). The body curves inwards before a short, everted foot (height 3mm). It is divided into five enamelled zones. From the top, they are as follows:

- a reserved olive or laurel wreath on an enamelled background (the upper part blue, the lower green), its borders with serrated edges;

- a reserved zig-zag on a red background;

- a sinuous vegetal scroll of ten alternating ivy leaves on a blue background, the stalk and tendrils reserved, the leaves green and blue. The edges of the zone are serrated, and this is also used within the design to evoke a leaf-like appearance;

- another reserved zig-zag on red;

- a vandyked band at the base with blue pendant triangles. The reserved motif is not strictly triangular, but is analogous to the flanking lines in the leaf scroll discussed below, with paired notches cut into its edges.

The casting is technically excellent, with only a few hints of casting flaws: on the olive wreath, at two points on the lower part (at around 100° and 135°) the lower leaf of the pair is missing, while in the upper zig-zag band a short section is missing at about 45°. On the lowest zone, in places the reserved motifs do not reach the top of the field.

The vegetal scroll is worth describing in detail, as it is a careful and subtle design (Figure 9.1b). The sinuous stalk has ten alternating ivy leaves; the stalk thickens at each leaf, where it is serrated on one side, with two angled cuts defining the bud of the leaf on the other. The leaf has a rounded base and tapers to a tip, its outer edges serrated. At the base is an inner circle which has a reserved oval at the junction with the stalk and four conjoined hemispheres on the opposite, outer edge. A reserved double-pointed line runs down the centre of the tip; opposed V-notches are cut into it around midway. A similar double-point motif lies between the leaf and the stalk on alternate, downward-pointing leaves. From the base of each leaf, a tendril curls backwards; it bifurcates into a thick comma-scroll curled into the stalk and a thin lobe curled out. There are two exceptions, both in the upper field; at 90°, the tendril has only a single scroll, and does not bifurcate; under the handle, the motif is more complex, with a thick comma scroll curling forward and a secondary tendril curling back and splitting in two (Figure 9.1c). The line between leaf and stalk is also more complex, being a three-line zig-zag rather than a single line. This deliberate asymmetry lies at the point where the handle was attached, suggesting this marks the start and finish of the design.

The handle has a sinuous expanded terminal and leaf-like volutes either side of its attachment to the bowl (Figure 9.1d). It bears a linear leaf design. Two ivy leaves are set in a line; they differ markedly in detail, but both have tendrils coiling off each side near the tip, bifurcating into a comma scroll and cusp. This leaf-line ends at a semi-circle enclosing a small double-leaf motif. The handle is predominantly enamelled in blue, with outlines of the leaves and the semi-circle in red, and the heart of the leaves in green; reserved areas set off the design.

Overall length 208mm; external rim diameter 113mm; maximum diameter 117.5mm; base diameter 62-65mm; height 67mm; handle length (to rim) 92mm, width 27mm (minimum), 49mm (terminal), 97mm (between ends on rim). Surface X-ray fluorescence analysis by Susy Kirk (NMS Analytical Research Section) showed that both bowl and handle were made of a leaded bronze (*c.* 13% tin and 2% lead), with the replacement base being of a modern brass. The red enamel had been coloured with copper, the blue with cobalt and the green with copper and lead.

AN ENAMELLED HANDLE FROM AN IRON AGE SITE AT ARDOWNIE, ANGUS

The West Lothian Pan has long been known, but a more recent find adds fresh impetus to study of the type. This enamelled handle was found by CFA Archaeology in 2001 while excavating a substantial souterrain (an underground stone-built passage, probably a cellar, typical of the local Iron Age) at Ardownie, near Dundee. The site, and the find, are fully published (Anderson & Rees 2006; Hunter 2006); this account is, therefore, a summary. The handle is detached from its bowl, and has broken around mid-shank, been repaired, and broken again. The terminals at the bowl end are in the form of birds' heads. The decoration is naturalistic: a hunting dog is in eager pursuit of two hares, which run to the corners of the handle. A crescent above the dog's muzzle may represent the moon; there is also a small reserved rectangle below its throat and a pellet between the hares.

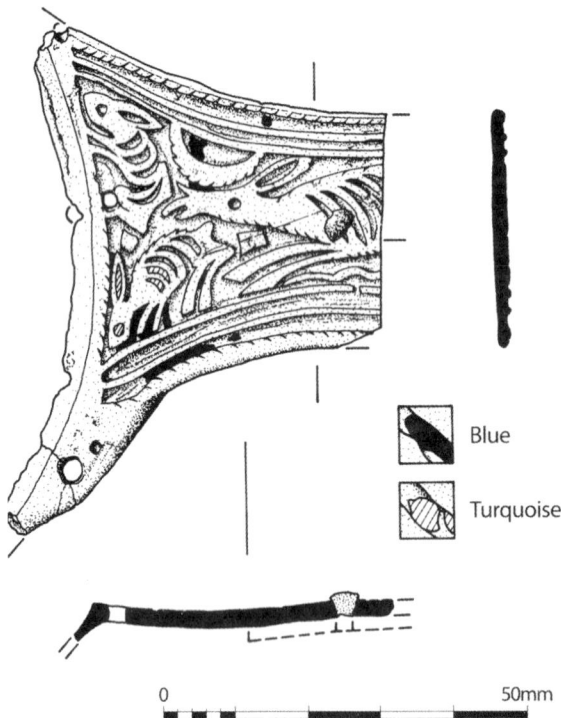

Blue

Turquoise

0   50mm

Figure 9.3. The Ardownie handle

Enamelling is mostly lost, but was in blue and turquoise. Alloy: leaded bronze with minor zinc. Surviving length 53mm, width 66mm, thickness 3-5mm; vessel diameter *c.* 115mm.

TYPES AND TYPOLOGIES

What do these old and new finds add to the topic of this volume? New finds are of particular value in broadening our picture of enamelled vessels, which has long been dominated by relatively few well-known objects. What follows very much builds on the work of others, especially Henry (1933), Moore (1978), Bateson (1981, 50-53), Künzl (1995 and this volume) and Jackson (this volume), but it is perhaps of value to have some synthesis of a scattered field. Recently-published material from northern England has allowed re-evaluation of the range of enamelled vessels, with finds of near-intact vessels from Catterick and Corbridge enabling many nondescript fragments to be

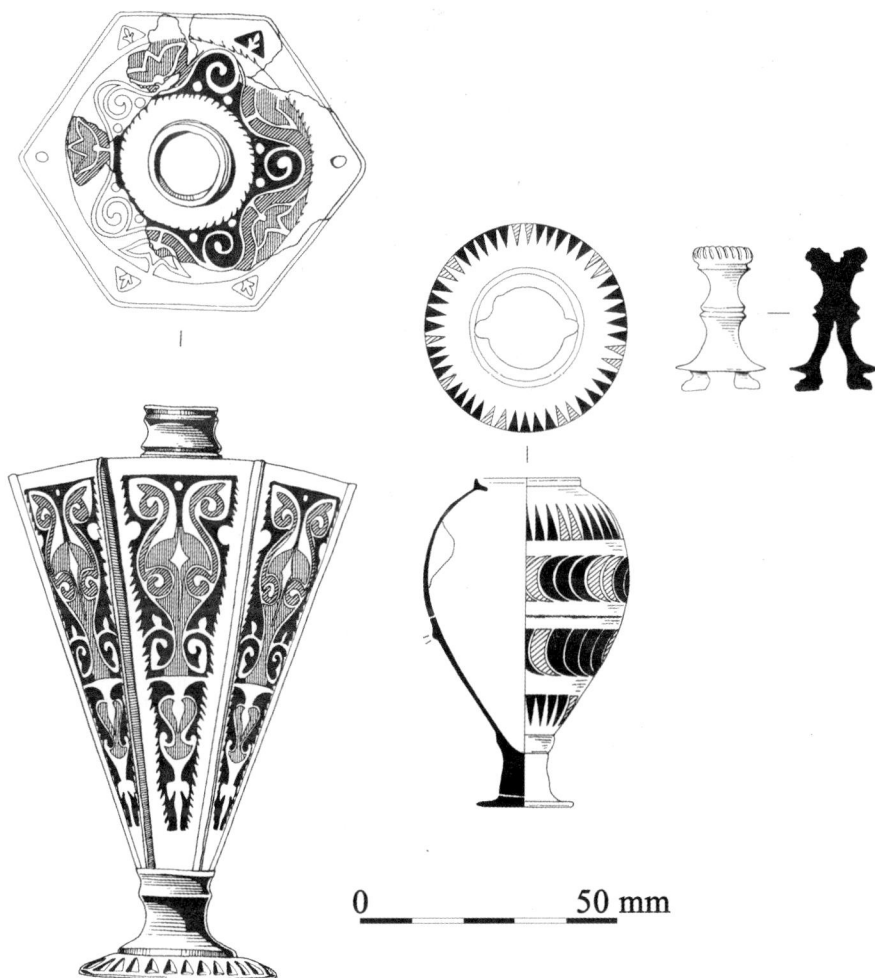

Figure 9.4. The flasks from Corbridge (left) and Catterick (from Casey & Hoffmann 1995, 24; Allason-Jones 2002, fig. 268)

interpreted more fully. Recent finds of enamelled pans have also expanded our understanding substantially beyond the three types which have been emblematic since the work of Moore (1978).

To take the broader picture first, as Künzl (this volume) indicates, a wide range of large enamelled items, especially, but not exclusively, vessels, was produced within the Roman province of Britain and the near Continent in the late first and second centuries. The pans have long been recognised as a series, but many others appeared near-unique items until recently; however, other coherent types can now be recognised. The Castleford (Yorkshire) mould fragments confirmed the manufacture of enamelled vessels in Britain, notably cylindrical flasks, while two further distinctive types can now be defined: small footed flasks with oval bodies and elongated necks, and small footed flasks with hexagonal-sectioned tapering bodies (Figure 9.4).

The key for the oval flasks was the find from Catterick (Yorkshire). In publishing this, Allason-Jones (2002) drew together a range of material from Britain and the near Continent, linked not only by form but decoration, which is dominated by rows of triangular or sinuous-triangular cells. At least six examples can now be identified: from Catterick and Housesteads (UK), Mook (NL), Mönchengladbach (D), Famars (F), and one unprovenanced (Allason-Jones 2002; 2009, 438, fig 14.5 no 50; den Boesterd 1956, no 307; Louvre Br. 3128; Henry 1933, fig 43.3 = Fitzwilliam GR.29.1904). For hexagonal flasks, the find from a cremation on the Corbridge bypass was the key (Casey and Hoffmann 1995, 24; Cool 2006, 67). These vessels were made up of separate tops, bases, and six body panels, and the dissociated components were hard to identify, but this discovery allowed re-identification of finds from Ivy Chimneys, Silchester, Aldborough, Carmarthen, and probably Dinorben as examples of the type (Webster 1999, 88, fig. 60; Henry 1933, fig. 46.2; Bishop 1996, 94, no. 605; James 2003, 317-8, fig. 8.4 no. 57; Gardner & Savory 1964, 148-9, fig. 19.10, pl. XXXIV (a) no. 4); there is also an unpublished panel fragment from Vindolanda (noted in site museum), and Worrell (this volume) reports a further fragment from Sutton (Suffolk), while intact examples are known in Bonn (Henry 1933, pl. 2), Gorgippia (Ukraine; Alekseeva 1993; Leskow *et al.* 1989, 185, no. 269, Taf. 49) and in an American private collection, unusually with millefiori decoration (True & Hamma 1994, no. 165). This type is of particular interest as the decoration shows strong influences from Celtic art (see below).

These freshly-recognised forms emphasise the broad range of enamelled vessels, although handled pans still dominate (Figure 9.5). Assuming the pans were in some sense culinary, they find companions in a less frequent range of beakers (both open and closed forms; e.g. from Benevento (Italy), Selborne (UK), and a minor component among the Castleford moulds; Henry 1933, fig. 23.1; R Jackson *pers. comm.*; Bayley & Budd 1998, 212-4, patterns 9-13), single finds of vases and buckets (Henry 1933, fig. 24.4;

Food and drink

Hand-washing (at table or rituals)

Perfume flasks

Ink wells

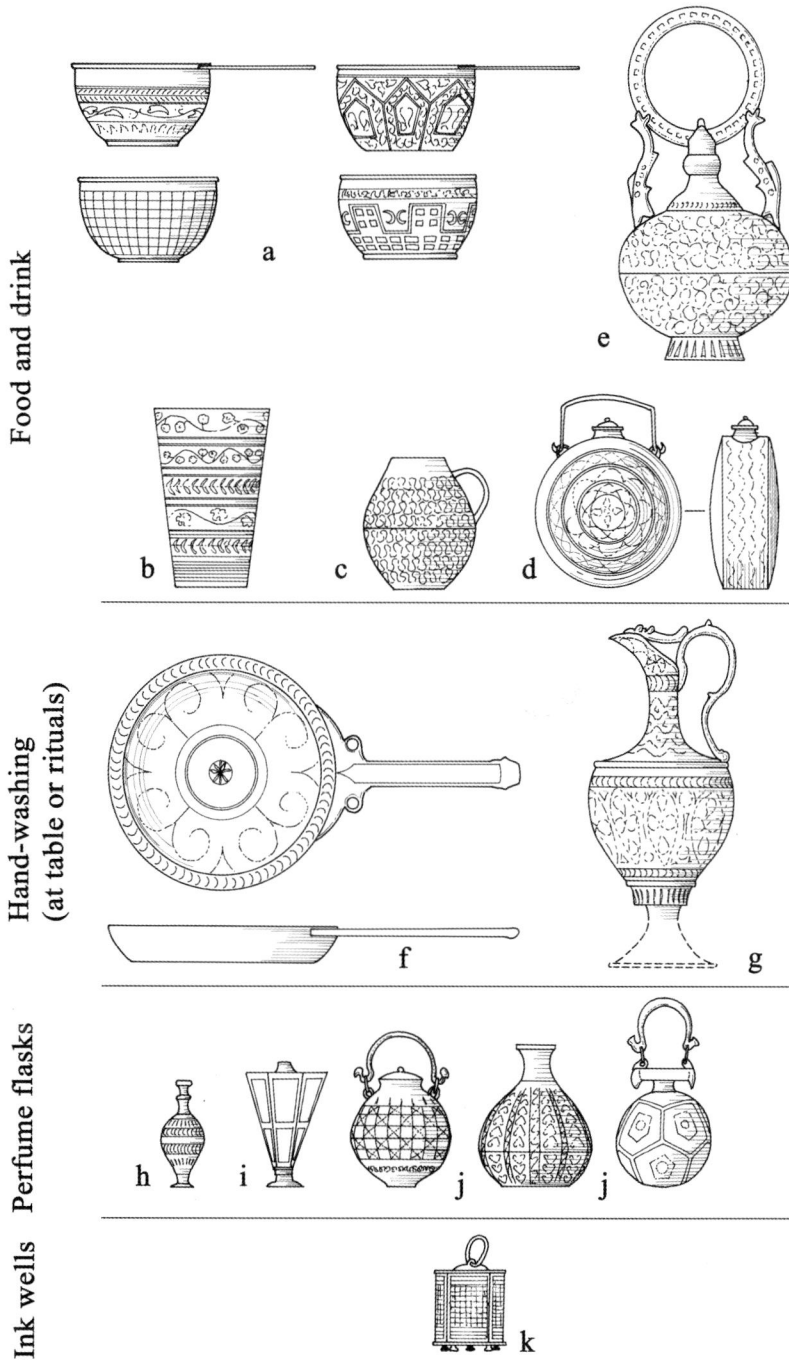

Figure 9.5. The main types of enamelled vessels; a. handled pan; b. open beaker; c. closed beaker; d. cylindrical flask; e. 'wine thief'; f. patera; g. jug; h. oval flask; i. hexagonal flask; j. various toilet flasks; k. ink well

Forsyth 1950, 298), and large flasks, including what Bailey (2003) identifies as a 'wine thief' from Ambleteuse (F), with a perforated base and a small hole in the top for withdrawing liquid from a larger vessel using surface tension. The cylindrical flasks known from Pinquente (Istria, Croatia) (Figure 2.3) and Bélgida (Spain: Henry 1933, pl. 1; Anon. 1990, 293, no. 246) and as moulds from Castleford are probably linked to the consumption of drink, given their resemblance to military field flasks (eg Close-Brooks 1977-78). The jug and patera set now in Mainz may be related to the washing of hands at table or before rituals. Many of the other vessels are connected with personal hygiene in some sense, with a range of flasks most plausibly for oils, ointments or perfumes (see discussion in Koster 1997, 82); to this might be added the few known strigils (e.g. Künzl 1995, 46; McCarthy 1990, 119, fig. 108 no. 45, wrongly identified as a belt slide). Cultural life is represented also by the hexagonal pyxides, probably inkwells (Künzl 1995, 46; Forsyth 1950, fig. 1-3).

The Ilam Pan, the inspiration for this book, impacts on the typology of the enamelled pan series. As Jackson notes in this volume, there was clearly a pick-and-mix approach to stylistic traits in the manufacture of such vessels, demonstrating close links between the various members and suggesting closely-linked workshops, but creating a bit of a nightmare for would-be typologisers. It is worth saying, however, that Moore's (1978) three-fold division of the pans is too simple: the number of exceptions has become a significant proportion of the total. We could simply add categories: the chequerboard pattern long known from Bingen (Germany) is now paralleled

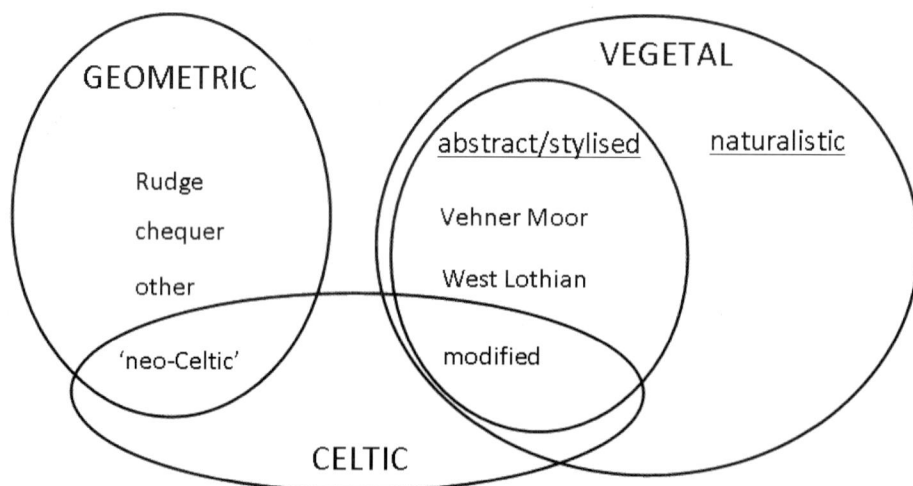

Figure 9.6. A Venn diagram approach to categorising the decoration on enamelled vessels (millefiori decoration is omitted as it is unconnected with the others)

at Winterton (Lincs. UK; Worrell, this volume, Figure 8.1), and a category of handles with hunt scenes can be identified. However, a broader view is needed (Figure 9.6). Rather than defining specific types, it is perhaps more useful to define four major decorative palettes which were being used: vegetal, geometric, Celtic-influenced, and millefiori. This sees the Vehner Moor/pentagon pattern as a variant of vegetal decoration, and bundles the chequerboard and crenellated/Rudge-type pans along with objects such as oval flasks, in having a design based on repeated simple shapes. Within the vegetal category, one could go further; for instance, rather than differentiating Vehner Moor and West Lothian styles, it may be better to treat these sinuous, almost abstract designs as one vegetal tradition, differentiated from a more naturalistic tradition represented by the beaker from Benevento (Italy) and the unprovenanced vessels from the Fitzwilliam and Metropolitan Museums (Henry 1933, fig. 23.1, 24.4; Forsyth 1950, fig. 7-9). However, while there is a validity in this, it risks becoming over-compartmentalised: the sharing of motifs on which Jackson comments, and indeed the diversity in the Castleford workshop (with examples of all styles apart from millefiori; Bayley & Budd 1998, 219, who split the vegetal group in two) shows that straightforward typological analysis has its limits.

Table 9.1 shows the main associations on a single vessel between these

Table 9.1. Co-occurrence of key design elements on single vessels. Descriptive rather than the traditional findspot terms are preferred for the types.

Decoration	1	2	3	4	5	6	7	8	9	10
1 Vegetal ('West Lothian')	X	4	4	3	9	6				1
2 Pentagonal ('Vehner Moor / Bad Pyrmont')		X			1					
3 Crenellated ('Rudge')			X	1	2	1	1			
4 Chequerboard ('Bingen')				X	1					
5 Other geometric					X		1			
6 Neo-Celtic						X				
7 Running wave / meander							X			
8 Hunt scene								X		
9 Millefiori									X	
10 Other										X

major decorative styles; some links are between vessel bodies and handles, others on the same vessel body. Table 9.2 divides this by vessel type, which emphasises the interconnectedness of types and the separateness of millefiori decoration. This supports Künzl's arguments (1995, 46) for a different workshop tradition for millefiori; it occurs on different vessel types, with the exception of a single millefiori-decorated hexagonal flask (True & Hamma 1994, no. 165), a type which more typically bears vegetal and Celtic ornament (see below).

Table 9.2. Correlation between vessel type and decorative style. Note that the right-hand column is the total number of vessels, not the sum of the preceding columns (as some vessels have several decorative styles and others are not illustrated adequately). Similar styles are also found on non-vessels, such as candlesticks, plaques and strigils, but these are not considered here.

	Vegetal			Geometric			Mille-fiori	Celtic	Other			No.
	W Lothian scroll	Penta-gonal	Other naturalistic	Crene-llated	Chequer	Other			Scroll	Hunt	Other	
Pan/handle	8/11	7/0	–	4	2	2/1	–	1	2/4	0/4	1	22/21 (total 37)
Flask, ovoid						6						6
Flask, hexa-gonal	4					1	1	7				11
Flask, cylind-rical	2				2	1		1				3
Flask, large	3			1	1	6		1				7
Beaker			1					2				3
Inkwell							13					13
Cockerel					1	6						7
Other vessel	4	1	2		3	6	1	8				18
No.												105

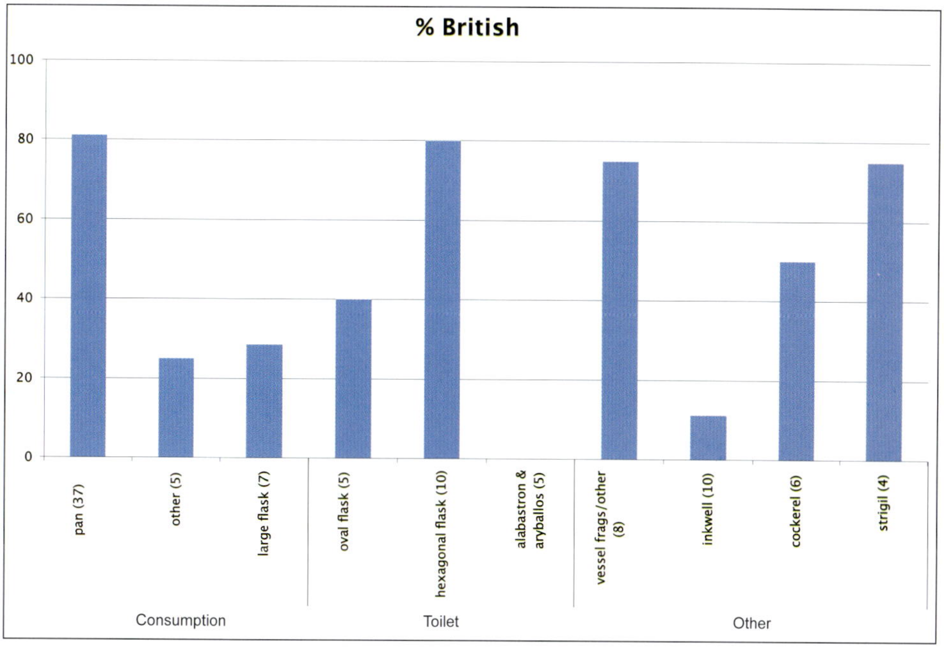

Figure 9.7. Proportion of different vessel types with British provenances. Unprovenanced vessels are not included

Figure 9.8. Fragment from a flask or other bipartite vessel from Great Chesterford, Essex

Table 9.2 shows that some styles were shared between vessel types, but others were more restricted. This may in part be for practical reasons – the pentagonal motif requires vessels of a certain scale, for instance, and would be hard to squeeze on a small flask – but it also suggests a variety of workshops, and a dominance of enamelled pans as the main (and most varied) product. As Künzl's map indicates (1995, Abb. 6), such vessels were distributed very broadly. His fig. 6 shows what proportion of different functional categories are found in Britain: pans, hexagonal flasks and strigils (the latter from a small sample) are predominantly British, but others are as or more common outside Roman Britain (Figure 9.7). Künzl's 'neo-Celtic' style is poorly represented in Britain, with only two known fragments, from Halton Chesters and Great Chesterford (Figure 9.8). On the basis of distribution one might prefer a French source, given the discoveries from Ambleteuse, La Guierche and the Mainz 'north French' find, but the Castleford find shows the danger of such distributional arguments; mould pattern 17 (Bayley & Budd 1998, 216) is of this style.

CELTIC AND NEO-CELTIC

The striking decoration on the Ilam Pan, with its roundels with triple-comma swirls and triskeles, leads us to consideration of motifs characteristic of Celtic art on this group of material. Künzl (1995) has already defined a 'neo-Celtic' category, based on the jug and *patera* set now in Mainz, while the hexagonal flasks noted above provide further examples. Decoration influenced by Celtic art can be seen on a number of vessels, but this does not represent the simple application of pre-existing motifs to new forms; instead, what we see is creative adaptation of the art to new influences and objects. This ability to incorporate and adapt new influences creatively is often argued as a key feature of Celtic art in long-term perspective (Megaw & Megaw 2001, 20-21). Recent years have seen extensive debate over the use of the term 'Celtic', and one must be careful to avoid any perceived ethnic significance to it; Iron Age communities in Europe show both connections and divergences, and to lump them under a single term is a gross over-simplification. In the case of the art, however, we can recognise elements of a common tradition, albeit with considerable diachronic variation, and it can be seen on these vessels. This is sometimes termed La Tène-style decoration rather than Celtic, though this too is problematic in its assumption of origins. Celtic is used here as shorthand for recognisable influences from British indigenous art (see Garrow 2008, 17).

VEGETAL DECORATION

Of the major decorative palettes defined above, vegetal, geometric and Celtic-influenced are most relevant here. In fact, material showing Celtic decoration can be seen as interpretations of vegetal or geometric ornament: it is not a separate category, but a different response. Let us start with vegetal decoration, and consider where Celtic influences can be recognised. Three main vessel groups are of relevance: hexagonal flasks, the Ilam Pan, and a series of vessels with complex compass-based ornament. A few other finds will be considered as we progress.

Hexagonal flasks form a good starting point, as they illustrate a key feature of this decoration: the integration of Classical motifs and indigenous interpretations (Figure 9.4). The top of the flask has a Classical vegetal leaf scroll around the neck. Each panel of the body has a symmetrical vegetal design, differing slightly in detail between vessels, but typically with two zones, the lower dominated by a sinuous leaf-pair springing from a pelta, the upper with a scroll pattern including trumpet motifs and comma scrolls with cusps, typical designs from Celtic art. (The two continental finds, Gorgippia and the unprovenanced vessel now in Bonn, have more classically vegetal decoration, suggesting this may have been preferred by the export market.)

The decoration on the Ilam pan is discussed in detail by Jackson (this volume), who stresses Celtic elements such as the comma swirl and the triskele, and notes parallels in particular to Mirror-style art from southern England in the immediately pre-Roman period. The roundels and triskeles catch our eye today, but this may not have been so clear in Roman times; when complete, enamelling would have blurred this division, with fields of the same colour both inside and outside the roundels. This would add to the sense of movement in the design, leading the eye from one roundel to the next and drawing attention to another aspect: with its reserved tendrils and elongated fields with serrated edges, the design can be read as a more Classical vegetal scroll. Different onlookers might even interpret the design differently, as more Celtic or more Classical, according to their own aesthetic sensitivities (cf. F. Hunter 2008, 142).

Such readings focus on typically 'Celtic' or 'Classical' motifs. However, Ilam leads us towards another approach. In reading the roundels as a vegetal scroll, this springs from leaf-tip to leaf-tip rather than the leaves springing from a stalk as in a true classical version. Similar features have been noted by other writers: Henry (1933, 110-4), in describing the enamelled 'altar plaque' from the Thames, talks of 'a very free adaptation of the Roman ivy leaf', while on the Elmswell plaque, Corder and Hawkes (1940, 355-6) comment on scrolls springing from the leaves and extra trumpet scrolls on the ends of the enamelled portion, noting 'the Roman is indeed celticized in certain details' (Figure 9.9). This non-naturalistic treatment of vegetal patterns, especially with scrolls developing from leaves, is seen also on the handle of the West Lothian Pan, the handles from Burgh Apton and Kirkby Lathorpe (Moore 1978, figs. 1 and 4), and the lid of the perfume flask from Camarina (Italy; di Vita et al. 1995, fig. 27). Sometimes indigenous influence is seen not in style but layout: Fowler (1983, 237) notes that the leaf design in the Bradley Hill pentagons forms a lyre-palmette typical of Celtic art, and this is seen also on the Thames plaque (Henry 1933, figs. 24.5, 26.1). The enamelled item from Droitwich (Worcs; Lloyd-Morgan 2006, 66-7, fig. 44 no. 6), probably a strigil handle, is a variant on the same theme, a less successful fusion of styles, but with the four conjoined roundels representing a vegetal scroll containing trumpet-based leaf motifs. It expands the range of objects to which this 'neo-Celtic' style was applied.

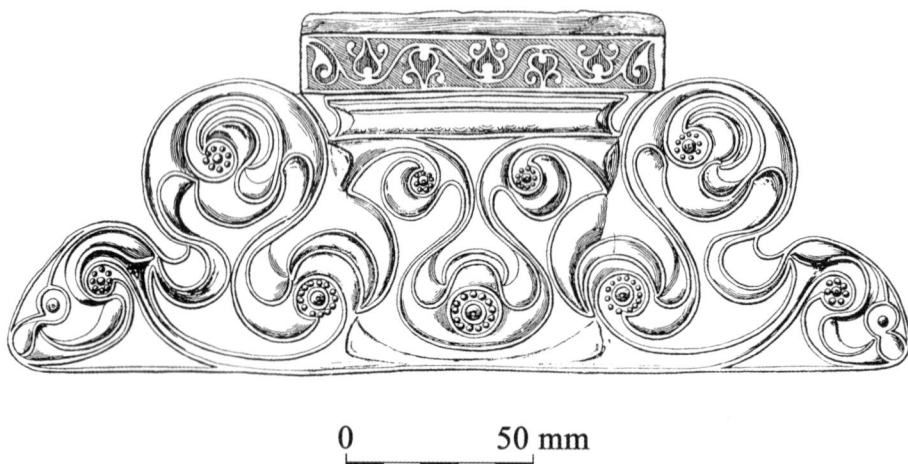

0   50 mm

Figure 9.9. The Elmswell plaque (Jope 2000, pl. 222b)

Such non-naturalistic treatment of vegetation would traditionally be seen as provincial in a derogatory sense, unable to reach the heights of true classical art. Yet this is to underrate the intentions of the artist. Exactly such a conversion from Mediterranean naturalism to 'the Celtic abstract' is seen in the Vegetal or Waldalgesheim style of the fourth century BC, and widely hailed as an artistic highpoint (Megaw & Megaw 2001, 108-21). This is not to argue for some elusive 'Celtic spirit' over half a millennium in widely different parts of Europe, but to note that the creative adaptation of classical art has a long pedigree; these enamelled vessels are a fine example.

The final group of material, epitomised by the Mainz washing set, is rather different (Künzl 1995; 2009). Here, interlocking compass-based ornament dominates. This seems very close to the rather less regular *Trompetenmuster* designs, most common in the later second and third centuries (MacGregor 1976, 186-9); the Castleford evidence indicates its currency from *c.* 85-100 (Bayley & Budd 1998, 216, fig. 90). On the Mainz jug, in particular, typical Celtic motifs can be recognised: reserved trumpets (often conjoined) and enamelled trumpet voids, yin-yang circles, short comma-spirals and so forth.

The accompanying pan lacks such clear elements, being more geometric with its running waves, crescents and leaf motifs, but as Künzl (1995, 41) notes, the stylised animals at the junction of handle and bowl, defined by trumpets, are typical of British late Iron Age art. Künzl (1995, 42) links other vessels to this style, such as the 'wine-thief' from Ambleteuse and the flask from La Guierche (both France); he also puts containers in the form of cockerels into this group, but the examples I know have more repetitively geometric motifs, such as lozenges and crescents, and they are treated here with the geometric group.

These groups of materials show a blending of interpretations; the Mainz set with more strictly geometric compass-based designs, the hexagonal flasks using symmetrical scrolls, and the Ilam pan sharing elements of both. Whence do the influences come? It is noteworthy that, while individual elements find ready parallels, one struggles to find precise parallels for the designs: these objects represent creative adaptations to new influences. For compass-based designs, one can look to southern British Mirror style, as Jackson (this volume) suggests, and to the more flowing, more vegetal enamelling also found in the south on horse harness (e.g. Jope 2000, pl. 292-3). This makes it tempting to look to the south for inspiration, following in the footsteps of earlier scholars who often saw refugees from the south bringing these skills to the north (Corder & Hawkes 1940, 353-4; Moore 1978, 325; MacGregor 1976, 178-181). The Roman conquest, of course, had major impacts on indigenous societies, but in recent years such diffusionist explanations have jarred as researchers understand better the complexity of the northern societies without a reliance on southern influences. How do our southern craftworkers now fare? While the flowing enamel of the southern horse harness demonstrates an advanced technology of ambitious enamelling, it does not provide precise parallels for the designs. One can find compass-based ornament more widely across late Iron Age Britain, notably in the widespread series of openwork triskele roundels (where echoes of the Ilam roundels may be found; Jope 2000, pl. 225), and on a diffuse range of copper alloy, bone and pottery items across Britain and Ireland (e.g. Jope 2000, pl. 188-93, 226e-f, 228-9, 304-5, 316-7; MacGregor 1976, nos. 274-5). So-called 'Casket Ornament' (Jope 2000, pl. 222-4), starting just before the Roman period and flourishing during it (Macdonald 2007a, 146-151), is also relevant: its best examples show flowing compass-based Celtic design. Most striking here is the Elmswell (Yorks, UK) plaque (Figure 9.9), with a narrow panel of enamelled classically-inspired leaf-scroll, similar to many of the enamelled pans, and a broad sheetwork panel of flowing trumpet scrolls which echoes and reflects this in an indigenous style (Corder & Hawkes 1940; Jope 2000, pl. 222a-b). The analysis by Hawkes identifies valuable parallels, although today it reads as a message from a different world, where art styles and individual motifs could be tied to craft-workers from different tribes.

Perhaps current students of insular Celtic art have simply replaced this with uncertainty, but this seems more realistic (e.g. Macdonald 2007b); the link from art style to 'people' or 'tribe' is not demonstrated.

Where does this leave our influences? The evidence of production, partial as it is, points to northern and western Britain, with the best evidence being the moulds from Castleford and, probably, Caerleon (Bayley & Budd 1998; Boon 1986). Although influences from Celtic art can be seen across Roman Britain, notably in brooch types, they are especially prevalent in the north and west, as Collingwood (1930) long ago commented. Caution may be our best policy in trying to identify lineages here, since the manufacturers were not slavishly following their earlier styles but creatively adapting a canon. There is no need to posit a southern origin; while it is possible, this very creativity makes it rather superfluous to attempt to follow such stylistic trends. Rather, it represents a broader habit of adaptation. This contrasts with other hybrid Romano-British styles, where pre-existing patterns were applied to Roman forms (such as swash-N motifs on seal boxes or military belt-plates; F. Hunter 2008, table 8.1). Instead, here we see a truly hybrid art, taking the inspiration of Classical forms of vegetal scroll and developing them in the local idiom, which itself was transformed in the process. In the finest examples, one sees the two in deliberate contrast as at Elmswell, or integrated as at Ilam, where I would argue that the traditions are successfully fused, with different viewers able to prioritise different elements. These vessels are thus a very potent example of the complexity of cultural interchange in Britain, and show considerable artistic innovation during the second century, a contrast to R. G. Collingwood's rather dismissive appraisal of Romano-British art (Collingwood and Myres 1937, 249).

Geometric decoration

The geometric decoration found on many vessels can also be viewed from an indigenous perspective. Celtic art in central Britain and Wales shows exactly such small-cell enamelling, typically bichrome, in both squares and triangles, in the late pre-Roman and Roman Iron Age (e.g. MacGregor 1976, 184; Davis & Gwilt 2008). Table 9.3 provides an indication of the frequency with which different motifs were used on these vessels: triangles, crescents and squares, well-known from indigenous enamelling, dominate. There are also rarer motifs which are found in indigenous Celtic art: the pelta (ultimately classical) and the quatrefoil. This geometric decoration may lack the visibly 'Celtic' element, in Garrow's sense of 'swirly art' (2008, 18), and was in no sense unique to this area, but it was clearly consistent both technically and aesthetically with indigenous tradition, and was applied to the new forms of cast bronze vessels.

In sum, we can recognise several decorative strands within this group of

Table 9.3. Frequency of specific geometric motifs on enamelled vessels. As it is based primarily on published illustrations, some motifs will inevitably be overlooked; a couple of vessels are excluded as no images were available. The 'other' column comprises solely single instances.

Vessel	△	◇	(	☾	ʒ	□	✸	Other
Pan	5	1		4	2	5	1	diagonal lines, square with triangular top
Flask, ovoid	5		5	1				zig-zag
Flask, hexagonal	2							
Flask, cylindrical	3	1		1		1	1	circle, herringbone
Flask, large	4			2		1		oval
Cockerel	1	2		4		1		
Other vessel	6	3		3		1		
Number	26	7	5	15	2	9	2	6

material with Celtic design influences, but no exact genealogies to earlier styles. This was no straightforward dropping of existing styles onto new forms, but a creative reinterpretation in the light of fresh influences, leading, in the best cases, to highly original and innovative works of art. It serves to highlight very eloquently the cultural processes of hybridisation on the frontier.

BEYOND THE FRONTIER

The final area to comment on here is the desirability of this material in societies beyond the imperial frontier; some ten per cent of known finds come from beyond the Empire. From wealthy graves around the Black Sea, at Kertsch and Gorgippia in the Crimea (Künzl 1995, 46), through Germanic groups in the Czech Republic, Poland, Germany and Denmark, to the frontier lands of Scotland, these vessels were desirable. In the debatable lands between the Walls of Hadrian and Antoninus, finds such as West Lothian and Harwood (Henry 1933, fig. 27.11) exist in an interpretative limbo; it is unclear if they are best seen as finds from beyond the frontier or within the province. Indeed, drawing such 'frontier lines' can be misleading: the find from Dinorben, a north Welsh hillfort, in many senses is more similar to areas beyond than within the frontier. The Ardownie find tells a clearer story: from an Iron Age site north of the Antonine Wall, it clearly shows the desirability of such items in indigenous societies. Yet it is unusual beyond the frontier because it is a fragmentary settlement find. These are increasingly recognised within the

Empire, and especially within *Britannia* thanks to the Portable Antiquities Scheme (Worrell, this volume), but finds from beyond the frontier are otherwise all from non-domestic contexts: burials or other ritual deposits. This emphasises the value placed on these items in local society.

There are regional patterns of preference. The Black Sea finds show a strong classical taste: an inkwell from Kertsch, an alabastron and strigil from Gorgippia (Künzl 1995). The Dutch find from Born-Buchten (Groningen) also reflects local preferences: it is a cockerel, fitting the unusual but strong north Netherlands tradition of obtaining and depositing Roman statuettes (e.g. Galestin 2000). Elsewhere beyond the northern frontiers, from Scotland to the Czech Republic, the preference was for enamelled pans. Sometimes other vessels were adapted to this form. Moore (1978, 326-7) suggests the Harwood vessel may have been cut down from a casket, though it may simply be the lower half of either a casket or a flask (cf. Forsyth 1950, fig. 10). The vessel from Nehasitz in Bohemia (Czech Republic) similarly has an unusually shallow profile for a pan but is consistent with half of a casket which has been reused. Its context is not certain; it was reported as a settlement find, but has been reinterpreted as a burial (Exner 1938, 47-8, pl. 21.1, 22.1; Drobejar 1999, 20, pl. 18.4; Andrzejowski 2011, n. 27). Reuse of a casket is seen also in a remarkable third-century female burial from a Wielbark-culture gravefield at Jartypory in eastern Poland (Andrzejowski 2011). The excavator suggests this represents two beakers, one cannibalised to form a lid, but their shape and the neatness of fit suggest instead that they represent a casket with the neck portion deliberately removed. It was buried wrapped in an organic mat, and contained several charred hazelnuts and the fruits of the guilder rose (Andrzejowski 2011). Other elements in the burial included an unusual silver handle, evidence of rich clothing, and an atypical imported glass vessel.

Jackson (this volume) has noted that many of the finds from within Britain come from ritual contexts, and this is true also of those from beyond the frontier. The Ardownie fragment may be a deliberate deposit as part of rituals of abandonment (Hunter 2006, 30-1). Clearer examples are the pan from Bad Pyrmont (Lower Saxony, D) (Figure 2.6), found in a spring along with a quantity of brooches, and the moor finds from Vehner Moor (Lower Saxony, D) and Maltbæk (Jutland, DK) (Erdrich 2002, 50, 73, Taf. 126, 127.1; Lund Hansen 1987, 94-6, 429, fig. 35). The condition of the West Lothian Pan indicates it too is a wetland deposit.

These vessels thus provide evidence of high-value Roman imports arriving beyond the frontier, and show evidence of modification, long lives and important social roles. In the north-west provinces, the preference was for pans or other open forms of vessel, sometimes modified to achieve this; in the few eastern finds, a more diverse range is recorded. The sample is really too small for detailed comment, though it is interesting that none of the 'barbarian' finds, even in northern Britain, are of the neo-Celtic styles.

Conclusions

This paper has been a series of notes on a theme, inspired by the Ilam Pan and by other recent finds. Specific finds continue to pose problems, notably over provenance in the case of the West Lothian Pan, but recent discoveries have greatly expanded our knowledge of the typological and decorative repertoire of the manufacturers. Analysis of those decorative schemes showing indigenous influence emphasises the creativity of artisans, with innovative styles created in the reaction between Celtic and Classical idioms. The wide distribution of the types within the Empire shows how desirable they were at the time, as Künzl (this volume) notes, while their regular discovery beyond the frontier, often in unusual or exceptional deposits, shows how desirable they were there too. This intriguing and informative category of finds has much still to reveal.

Figure 9.10. The pan from Hockwold-cum-Wilton, Norfolk

ADDENDUM

At a late stage in publication I was able to access information on an important assemblage from Bulgaria purchased on the art market (Kabakchieva 2009): an enamelled globular oil flask and three strigils with enamelled handles, all clearly made as a set. The vessel has horizontal bands of decoration: a naturalistic vine-leaf scroll linked to the vessels from Benevento, the Fitzwilliam and Metropolitan Museums (Henry 1933, fig. 23.1, 24.4; Forsyth 1950, fig. 7-9) and bands of stylised leaves, wreathes and running scrolls. It is not included in the various tables above, but does not affect the analysis.

Appendix: recent finds of enamelled pans from Britain

Table 9.4. Finds of enamelled pans from Britain since Moore (1978) and Künzl (1995), excluding those noted by Worrell (this volume) and the Ilam Pan. Abbreviations: R, Roman; IA, Iron Age; m/d, metal-detected.

Findspot	County	Context	Object type	Notes	Ref
Ardownie	Angus	IA site	Handle – hunt scene	Repaired	Hunter 2006
Bancroft	Bucks	R site	Handle – hunt scene		Hylton & Zeepvat 1994, 315, fig. 149 no. 132
Caerleon	Gwent	R fortress	Mould for ?handle (vegetal)		Boon 1986
Cotswolds	Gloucs	R site	Handle – running wave	Metal-detecting find; few details	*Treasure Hunting* Aug 1993, 30
Gloucester, New Market Hall	Gloucs	R fort & town	Bowl – geometric scale-like ornament		Hassall & Rhodes 1974, 89, fig. 34.1
Hockwold-cum-Wilton	Norfolk	Stray	Vehner Moor bowl (handle lost; repair patch)	Metal-detecting find; fig. 9.10 NWHCM: 1979.294	Norwich Museum
Leicester, West Bridge	Leics	R site	Handle – vegetal		Clay 1994, 147, no. 41, fig. 75 (wrongly numbered 40)
London, Lloyds / Fenchurch St	Middlesex	Burial	Bowl – row of peltae below rim	Very small (D 48 mm); burial dates to 120-60	Bluer *et al* 2006, 152
Old Sleaford	Lincs	R site	Handle – vegetal (wreath)	Elsdon (1997, 191) notes that Kirkby Lathorpe find (Butcher 1977, 45) is from same area.	Elsdon 1997, 190
Scole	Norfolk	R site	Handle – hunt scene	Repaired & broken again; context mid-Antonine to late C3	Rogerson 1977, 140-2
Unprovenanced		Stray	Handle – hunt scene		British Museum P1994.4-4.
Upper Witham Valley	Lincs	R site	Handle – scroll decoration	Details unclear on published image	Jolliffe 2010, 151, pl. 8.10

Chapter 10

Conclusions

David J. Breeze

Tullie House Museum, Carlisle, is to be thanked and congratulated for arranging the display of the three pans associated with Hadrian's Wall at the museum during the Pilgrimage of Hadrian's Wall in 2009. This not only allowed the pans to be seen and compared by a large number of people, but the exhibition admirably complemented Ernst Künzl's lecture. Indeed, without the display, the idea to publish the lecture would never have formed and without that one article, the others would not have been published.

Exhibitions are well known as being catalysts for publications. In this case, the act of creating the publication has led to the first full catalogue of these items, new ideas on their date and purpose, and the bringing together of a range of complementary material. The fact that not all authors agree on the date and interpretation of the pans should be seen as a sign of strength, or at least as a challenge.

THE DATE OF THE PANS

It would appear that the Ilam Pan was the earliest of the vessels for two reasons: the Celtic decoration and because the names were engraved later, unlike those on the Amiens Patera and the Rudge Cup which were cast, while, as Ernst Künzl remarks, its decoration suggests that it was not made for a specific purpose, unlike the other pans which bear a motive interpreted as a representation of Hadrian's Wall. Determining absolute dates is more difficult. One of the problems is the nature of Hadrian's Wall itself. The pans record the fort names westwards from Great Chesters, which lies close to the central point of the Wall. This is the only fort in the stretch of the Wall originally built in stone which is named on a pan. All the forts westwards of Birdoswald were erected in the turf sector of the Wall. A start was made on replacing the Turf Wall in Hadrian's reign, but only about five miles was achieved, the remaining 25 miles not being rebuilt until the army returned from the Antonine Wall in the 160s (Breeze and Dobson 2000; Breeze 2012). It is for this reason that Ernst Künzl prefers a date in the second half of the second century for the manufacture of the pans. He finds it unlikely the pans would have been made to commemorate a wall of turf.

Paul Holder, however, argues that the Ilam Pan was probably made during the reign of Hadrian for two reasons. Firstly, because the name of *Aballava*/Burgh-by-Sands is not on the pan while *Coggabata*/Drumburgh is and this chimes with one interpretation of the archaeological evidence that the former fort had not yet been built on the Wall (Jones and Woolliscroft 2001, 118). It ignores, however, two other pieces of evidence: these are that the fort at Burgh-by-Sands lies astride the Wall, a feature known only in the earlier Hadrianic forts, while the discovery nearby of Hadrianic pottery in a civilian context implies the existence of a contemporary fort (Masser and Evans 2005, 61; Breeze and Woolliscroft 2009, 77). Further, we know little of the detailed history of the fort at Drumburgh. Secondly, Holder argues, because the name *vallum Aelium* would be more appropriate for a Hadrianic date. We can also add that the way that the names have been engraved on the Ilam Pan and not cast suggests it was made earlier than the Rudge Cup and Amiens Patera.

Künzl and Holder date the Rudge Cup and the Amiens Patera to the second half of the second century. Lindsay Allason-Jones prefers an early date for all the pans when the Wall was 'new and exciting' and when the turrets were still in use: many were abandoned later in the second century (Breeze and Dobson 2000). Jackson does not commit himself other than suggesting a date within the second century. It is not impossible, though perhaps unlikely, that the Ilam Pan was made during Hadrian's reign and the more developed vessels later in the second century on the return to Hadrian's Wall from the Antonine Wall when the turf section was rebuilt in stone.

Yet, we must acknowledge that we are trying to create a realistic picture from little evidence, as Jackson and Hunter remind us. The circumstantial evidence for a Hadrianic date for the fort at Burgh-by-Sands which sits astride the Wall makes it even more strange that *Aballava*/Burgh-by-Sands does not appear on the Ilam Pan.

WHERE WERE THE PANS MADE?

We cannot be certain in identifying where the pans were made, though there are pointers. Moulds for similar vessels have been found at Castleford, supporting Ernst Künzl's earlier suggestion that they were made in Britain. Lindsay Allason-Jones has gone further. She suggests that 'the inclusion, or not, of various forts seems to suggest the metalworker or metalworkers were aware of nuances of fort status, which might argue against the idea that the vessels were made at some distance from the Wall'. In that case, we have a specific workshop to discover in the vicinity of the Wall, perhaps, as Paul Holder suggests, in Carlisle. Further, the general similarities in the style of the Rudge Cup, Amiens Patera, Bath Pan and Hildburgh Fragment outweigh the differences, such as the wedge-shaped 'crenellations' on the Bath Pan and Hildburgh Fragment, and suggest that they were made in the same workshop but not all by the same craftsman.

Künzl and Holder suggest that the Ilam Pan was made by Draco but Jackson argues that craftsmen normally stamped their vessels and that Draco was therefore the owner. The fact that the inscription was cut into the Ilam Pan after its manufacture might be thought to argue in favour of Draco being the name of the purchaser.

WHO WERE THE PANS MADE FOR?

All contributors agree that the pans were made as souvenirs of Hadrian's Wall. The Rudge Cup, Amiens Patera and presumably also the Bath Pan depict Hadrian's Wall. It has traditionally been assumed that a series of towers (named 'turrets' on the Wall) with crenellations is depicted, but Allason-Jones and Jackson have suggested that the towers may rather be the north gates of the forts on the Wall, which would fit well with the naming of forts along the tops of the vessels. This proposal might also fit better with the evidence for towers on the early second-century Trajan's Column, and later second century Column of Marcus, both in Rome, which are shown either with hipped or ridged roofs. The form of the tops of the gate towers on Hadrian's Wall is not known, though they are often depicted as being flat while those at the reconstructed fort at the Saalburg in Germany were gable-ended.

Earlier ideas that the known pans were part of a set which covered all the Wall forts has been challenged with the discovery of the third pan recording forts in the western sector of the Wall, with none listing the eastern forts. Three pans, from the number that might

Figure 10.1. A tower on Trajan's Column, Rome

have been made, is, however, statistically insignificant. Paul Holder argues that the addition of the phrase *rigore vali Aeli Draconis* to the Ilam Pan detracts from the proposition that the pans were produced in sets. Further, two more pans would need to have been manufactured to complete a set embracing all the forts on the Wall.

It has been suggested that the pans were made for soldiers returning home. In fact, many soldiers on retirement probably stayed close to where they had served (Roxan 2000, 308). Nevertheless, some did return home and it is perhaps such veterans who would have valued souvenirs of the Wall.

Ernst Künzl states that the pans were made for illiterate people, though acknowledging that there is evidence for literacy in the Roman army. Indeed, the fourth-century writer Vegetius goes so far as to state that the army required literate soldiers and that recruits should be sought with some knowledge of short-hand writing, calculation and reckoning (Vegetius, *de re militari*, II, 19). Further, in a soldier's path to the centurionate, a knowledge of writing was clearly important, at least through the second century and into the third (Breeze 1974, 263-78). Alan Bowman has noted in regard to the Vindolanda writing-tablets that 'one of the most striking features of the frontier context is the depth, quality and quantity of literacy, which is the medium for organizing and conducting military control, administration, and social and economic life' (Bowman 2006, 88). It is likely therefore that a soldier buying one of the Hadrian's Wall pans would have been able to read the names. The implication of Künzl's point may be that the pans were made for civilians and, if so, which civilians would have bought them? The fact that all the pans have been found some distance from Hadrian's Wall lends support to Künzl's argument, and is given extra weight by the fact that most auxiliary soldiers appear to have remained near their base after retirement, as already noted (Roxan 2000, 308). It would appear that the fame of Hadrian's Wall was spread afar. In that context, we should note that vessels of this type are found beyond the Roman frontier so it is entirely possible that a pan depicting Hadrian's Wall may be found further north than the present range of discoveries.

What were the pans used for?

A souvenir can have uses over and above its primary purpose as a memento. It may have been bought to sit on the Roman equivalent of a mantelpiece, but the attachment of a handle to most pans argues that they had another role. If made for soldiers, that role could have related to ceremonies at retirement clubs. The find-spots of some of the pans are informative. The Bath Pan was found in the sacred springs in that city, the Rudge Cup in a well with some bones and Roman coins beside a Roman villa and the Amiens Patera in a house with a hypocaust and bath near the centre of the Roman city, all high-status places. The dedication to *Sulis Minerva* on the handle of the Bath Pan has led to the suggestion that the vessel was used in official rituals in the temple to the goddess. Bath was also a spa and pans have been found at temple-spa sites on the Continent such as Bad Pyrmont.

Jackson has emphasised that this link with water may be extended, for the Ilam Pan was found in a location overlooking the River Manifold at the place where it disappears into a sink-hole. These associations with water may not all be coincidental but may specifically relate for a final act of deposition, such as probably occurred with the West Lothian Pan.

It is impossible to know how long each of the pans was in use. Jackson has drawn attention to the evidence for long usage of one of the Bath pans, including heavy wear and repairs to the bowl and handle; its discoverer, Barry Cunliffe, suggested that it was deposited in the spring as a gift to the gods after its primary use had ended. The Ilam Pan has lost its handle and base as has the Rudge Cup; Allason-Jones notes that Horsley, writing in 1732, recorded the existence then of the base of the vessel. Other pans provide evidence for wear, damage and repair.

While final editing was in progress, Martin Henig published a typically thoughtful article on the pans (Henig 2010/11). In this he suggested that the pans were made in Carlisle, but he rejects their use as souvenirs, citing two objections: first, that such vessels usually have a religious context being designed for the pouring of libations, and, second, that travel in the ancient world was normally in order to undertake pilgrimages to religious sanctuaries and temples, and that a temple, possibly dedicated to Jupiter, may have existed at or near Carlisle. The pans may have been bought by pilgrims to the temple for use at their own cult centres at home. Henig also suggests that pilgrims to the temple could there, at the frontier of civilisation, invoke the gods who protected the Empire.

In conclusion, we may suggest that the pans were made on or beside Hadrian's Wall, most likely at Carlisle, in the second century, the Ilam Pan first and the others later, and sold as souvenirs, being used in religious ceremonies in places far removed from the Wall, some perhaps ending their lives as gifts to the gods.

Bibliography

E. M. Alekseeva, 'Gorgippia, cité du Bosphore', *Les Dossiers d'Archéologie* 188 (1993) 52-57

A. Alföldi, 'Chars funéraires bacchiques dans les provinces occidentales de l'empire Romain', *Antiquité Classique* 8 (1939) 347-359

M. R. Alföldi, *Bild und Bildersprache der römischen Kaiser. Beispiele und Analysen*. Kulturgeschichte der antiken Welt 81 (Mainz, 1999)

L. Allason-Jones, 'Enamelled flask from Catterick Bypass (Site 433)', in P. R. Wilson, *Cataractonium: Roman Catterick and its Hinterland. Excavations and Research, 1958-1997. Part II* (York, 2002) 78-80

L. Allason-Jones, 'The small finds', in A. Rushworth, *Housesteads Roman fort – The Grandest Station* (London, 2009) 430-87

D. Allen, *Roman Glass in Britain* (Princes Risborough, 1998)

J. Anderson, 'Notice of an enamelled cup or patera of bronze found in Linlithgowshire, recently purchased for the museum', *Proceedings of the Society of Antiquaries of Scotland* 19 (1885) 45-50

S. Anderson and A. R. Rees, 'The excavation of a large double-chambered souterrain at Ardownie Farm Cottages, Monifieth, Angus', *Tayside & Fife Archaeological Journal* 12 (2006) 14-60

J. Andrzejowski, 'Out of the social structure? A late Roman period female grave from Jartypory, eastern Poland', in D. Quast (ed), *Weibliche Eliten in der Frühgeschichte*. RGZM-Tagungen 10 (Mainz, 2011) 185-199

Anon., *A Guide to the Antiquities of Roman Britain in the Department of British and Medieval Antiquities* (London, 1922)

Anon., *Los Bronces Romanos en España* (Madrid, 1990)

B. Armbruster, 'Die Goldschmiedetechnik von Aržan 2', in: *Im Zeichen des goldenen Greifen. Königsgräber der Skythen* (München, 2007) 98-99

D. Bailey, 'A dandy dipper: the Ambleteuse clepsydra, Empedocles, and wine-thieves I have known', in C. Entwistle (ed), *Through a Glass Brightly. Studies in Byzantine and Medieval Art and Archaeology Presented to David Buckton* (Oxford, 2003) 1-9.

J. D. Bateson, *Enamel-working in Iron Age, Roman and Sub-Roman Britain*, BAR Brit. Ser. 93 (Oxford, 1981)

D. Bayard and J.-L. Massy, 1983 *Amiens Romain. Samarobriva Ambianorum. Revue Archéologique de Picardie* (Heilly, 1983)

J. Bayley, 'Spoon and Vessel Moulds from Castleford, Yorkshire', in S. T. A. M. Mols et al. (eds), *Ancient Bronzes. Acta of the 12th International Congress on Ancient Bronzes, Nijmegen 1992*. Nederlandse Archeologische Rapporten 18 (Amersfoort, 1995) 105-11

J. Bayley and P. Budd, 'The clay moulds', in: H. E. M. Cool and C. Philo (eds), *Roman Castleford I. The small finds*, Yorkshire Archaeology 4 (Wakefield, 1998) 195-222

P. Bidwell (ed), *Hadrian's Wall 1989-1999: a summary of recent excavations and research* (Kendal, 1999)

J. Bird, 'Catalogue of Iron Age and Roman artefacts discovered before 1995', in R. Poulton, 'Farley Heath Roman temple', *Surrey Archaeological Collections* 93 (2007) 1-147

E. Birley, *Research on Hadrian's Wall* (Kendal, 1961)

M. C. Bishop, *Finds from Roman Aldborough* (Oxford, 1996)

H. Blanck, *Das Buch in der Antike* (München, 1992)

R. Bluer, T. Brigham and R. Nielsen, *Roman and Later Development East of the Forum and Cornhill. Excavations at Lloyd's Register, 71 Fenchurch Street, City of London* (London, 2006)

G. C. Boon, 'A clay casting-mould', in J. D. Zienkiewicz, *The Legionary Fortress Baths at Caerleon II. The finds* (Cardiff, 1986) 218-19

G. C. Boon, Review of L. Allason-Jones and B. McKay, *Coventina's Well: a Shrine on Hadrian's Wall, Britannia* 19 (1988) 524-5

A. K. Bowman, 'Outposts of empire: Vindolanda, Egypt, and the empire of Rome', *Journal of Roman Archaeology* 19 (2006) 75-93

A. K. Bowman and J. D. Thomas, *The Vindolanda Writing-tablets (Tabulae Vindolandenses)* Volume II (London, 1994)

A. K. Bowman and J. D. Thomas, *The Vindolanda Writing-tablets (Tabulae Vindolandenses)* Volume III (London, 2003)

J. W. Brailsford, *Guide to the Antiquities of Roman Britain*, 3rd edn (London, 1964)

D. J. Breeze, 'The organization of the career structure of the *immunes* and *principales* of the Roman army', *Bonner Jahrbuch* 174 (1974) 245-92 = D. J. Breeze and B. Dobson, *Roman Officers and Frontiers* (Stuttgart, 1993) 11-58

D. J. Breeze, *J. Collingwood Bruce's Handbook to the Roman Wall*. 14th edn (Newcastle upon Tyne, 2006)

D. J. Breeze, 'The *civitas* stones and the building of Hadrian's Wall', *CW*[3] 12 (2012) 73-83

D. J. Breeze and B. Dobson, *Hadrian's Wall*, 4th edn (London, 2000)

D. J. Breeze and D. J. Woolliscroft (eds), *Excavation and Survey at Roman Burgh-by-Sands*, Cumbria Archaeological Research Reports 1 (Kendal, 2009)

D. Brown, 'Metal vessels', in B. Cunliffe (ed), *The Temple of Sulis Minerva at Bath, Vol. 2. The Finds from the Sacred Spring*. Oxford University Committee for Archaeology, Monograph 16 (Oxford, 1988) 14-21

J. C. Bruce, *A Descriptive Catalogue of Antiquities, chiefly British, at Alnwick Castle* (Newcastle upon Tyne, 1880)

W. Bulmer, 'Dragonesque Brooches and their development', *Antiquaries Journal* 18 (1938) 146-153

S. A. Butcher, 'Enamels from Roman Britain', in M. R. Apted, R. Gilyard-Beer and A. D. Saunders (eds), *Ancient Monuments and their Interpretation: essays presented to A. J. Taylor* (London, 1977) 41-70

W. Camden, *Britannia*, 5th edn (London, 1600)

R. Carr-Ellison, 'The Rudge Cup', *Archaeologia Aeliana* 2nd ser., 7 (1876) 262-5

P. J. Casey and B. Hoffmann, 'Excavations on the Corbridge Bypass, 1974', *Archaeologia Aeliana* 5th ser., 23 (1995) 17-45

R. Chevallier, *Roman Roads* (Berkeley and Los Angeles, 1976)

P. Clay, 'The small finds', in P. Clay and R. Pollard, *Iron Age and Roman Occupation in the West Bridge area, Leicester. Excavations 1962-1971* (Leicester 1994) 145-50

P. A. Clayton, 'Roman Bronze Bowl Depicts Map of Hadrian's Wall', *Minerva* 15 (2004) 1-4

J. Close-Brooks, 'A Roman iron flask from Newstead', *Proceedings of the Society of Antiquaries of Scotland* 109 (1977-8) 372-4

R. G. Collingwood, 'Romano-Celtic art in Northumbria', *Archaeologia* 80 (1930) 37-58

R. G. Collingwood and J. N. L. Myres, *Roman Britain and the English Settlements*, 2nd edn (Oxford, 1937)

P. Connolly, *The Roman Army* (London, 1975)

H. E. M. Cool, *The Roman Cemetery at Brougham, Cumbria. Excavations 1966-67*, Britannia Monograph Series 21 (London, 2004)

H. E. M. Cool, 'Additional comment' in D. F. Mackreth, 'Personal Ornaments', in J. Hughes, 'Hanbury Street, Droitwich: excavations 1980-82', in D. Hurst (ed), *Roman Droitwich* (York, 2006) 67

P. Corder and C. F. C. Hawkes, 'A panel of Celtic ornament from Elmswell, East Yorkshire', *Antiquaries Journal* 20 (1940) 338-57

J. D. Cowen and I. A. Richmond, 'The Rudge Cup', *Archaeologia Aeliana* 4th ser., 12 (1935) 310-342

B. Cunliffe (ed), *The Temple of Sulis Minerva at Bath, Vol. 2. The Finds from the Sacred Spring*. Oxford University Committee for Archaeology, Monograph 16 (Oxford, 1988)

J. Curle, 'An inventory of objects of Roman and provincial Roman origin found on sites in Scotland not definitely associated with Roman constructions', *Proceedings of the Society of Antiquaries of Scotland* 66 (1932) 277-397

M. Davis and A. Gwilt, 'Material, style and identity in first century AD metalwork, with particular reference to the Seven Sisters hoard', in D. Garrow, C. Gosden and J. D. Hill (eds), *Rethinking Celtic Art* (Oxford, 2008) 146-184

C. De Linas, 'Gourde antique en bronze émaillé', *Gazette Archéologique* (1884) 133-140

P. De Schaetzen and M. Vanderhoeven, 'De Romeinse lampen in Tongeren', *Het Oude Land van Loon*, XI (1956) 5- 31

M. H. P. den Boesterd, *The Bronze Vessels in the Rijksmuseum G. M. Kam at Nijmegen* (Nijmegen, 1956)

G. Di Stefano, 'Un triclinio per Afrodite', *Archeologia Viva* 14 nr. 52 nuova serie (1995) 26-31

A. Di Vita, G. Di Stefano and G. D'Andrea, *Camarina, Museo archeologico* (Palermo, 1995)

L. Dillemann, 'Observations on Chapter V. 31, Britannia, in the Ravenna Cosmography', *Archaeologia* 106 (1979) 61-73

M. Donderer, 'Merkwürdigkeiten im Umgang mit griechischer und lateinischer Schrift in der Antike', *Gymnasium* 102 (1995) 97-122

G. A. Drake, 'Percy, Algernon, Tenth Earl of Northumberland (1602-1668)', *Oxford Dictionary of National Biography* (Oxford, 2004-7)

E. Drobejar, *Od plaňanských pohárů k vinařické skupině (Kulturní a chronologické vztahy na území Čech v době římské a v časné době stěhování národů)* (= Sborník Národního Muzea v Praze/Acta Musei Nationalis Pragae A 53, 1-2 (Prague, 1999)

R. P. Duncan-Jones, 'Age-rounding, illiteracy and social differentiation in the Roman Empire', *Chiron* 7 (1977) 333-353

B. J. N. Edwards and D. J. Breeze, *The Pilgrimage of Hadrian's Wall 1999* (Kendal, 2000)

H. J. Eggers, *Der Römische Import im Freien Germanien* (Hamburg, 1951)

H. J. Eggers, 'Römische Bronzegefässe in Britannien', *Jahrbuch RGZM* 13 (1966) 67-164

S. M. Elsdon, *Old Sleaford Revealed. A Lincolnshire settlement in Iron Age, Roman, Saxon and Medieval times: excavations 1982-1995* (Oxford, 1997)

M. Erdrich, *Corpus der römischen Funde im europäischen Barbaricum: Deutschland Band 4. Hansestadt Bremen und Bundesland Niedersachsen* (Bonn, 2002)

K. Exner, 'Zwei römische Emailgefäße aus dem freien Germanien', in E. Sprockhoff (ed), *Marburger Studien: Gero Merhart von Bernegg gewidmet* (Darmstadt, 1938) 47-53

K. Exner, 'Das Verhältnis der pannonischen Emailfunde zu den rheinischen', in I. Sellye (ed), *Les Bronzes Emaillés de la Pannonie Romaine,* Diss. Pann. Ser. 2. Fasc. 8. (Budapest, 1939) 89-91

G. Faider-Feytmans, *Les Bronzes Romains de Belgique* (Mainz, 1979)

R. W. Feachem, 'Dragonesque Fibulae', *Antiquaries Journal* 31 (1951) 32-44

R. W. Feachem, 'Dragonesque Fibulae', *Antiquaries Journal* 48 (1968), 100-102

W. H. Forsyth, 'Provincial Roman enamels recently acquired by the Metropolitan Museum of Art', *The Art Bulletin* 32/4 (1950) 296-307

E. Fowler, 'A fragment of an enamelled bronze bowl from Bradley Hill, Somerton, Somerset', in A. O'Connor and D. V. Clarke (eds), *From the Stone Age to the 'Forty-Five* (Edinburgh, 1983) 237-42

A. W. Franks, 'A Roman enamelled cup found at Braughing...', *Proceedings of the Society of Antiquaries of London* 2nd ser., 4 (1870) 514-6

I. C. Freestone, C. P. Stapleton and V. Rigby, 'The production of red glass and enamel in the Late Iron Age, Roman and Byzantine periods', in C. Entwistle (ed), *Through a Glass Brightly. Studies in Byzantine and Medieval Art and Archaeology Presented to David Buckton* (Oxford, 2003)

S. S. Frere, *Britannia. A History of Roman Britain*, 3rd edn (London, 1987)

S. S. Frere and R. S. O. Tomlin (eds), *The Roman Inscriptions of Britain* Vol. II, fascicule 2 (*RIB* 2412-2420) (Oxford, 1991)

J. Gage, 'A letter ... communicating the recent discovery of Roman sepulchral relics in one of the greater Barrows at Bartlow, in the parish of Ashdon, in Essex', *Archaeologia* 26 (1836) 300-317

M. C. Galestin, 'Ensembles of Roman figural bronzes from the Netherlands', *Kölner Jahrbuch* 33 (2000) 143-50

W. Gardner and H. N. Savory, *Dinorben* (Cardiff, 1964)

D. Garrow, 'The space and time of Celtic art: interrogating the 'Technologies of Enchantment' database', in D. Garrow, C. Gosden and J. D. Hill (eds), *Rethinking Celtic Art* (Oxford, 2008) 15-39

T. Grane, *The Roman Empire and Southern Scandinavia – a Northern Connection* (Copenhagen, 2007)

K. Gschwantler, *Guss und Form. Bronzen aus der Antikensammlung* (Wien, 1986)

D. W. Harding, *The Archaeology of Celtic Art* (Abingdon, 2007)

M. McL. Harper, *Rambles in Galloway* (Edinburgh, 1876)

W. V. Harris, *Ancient Literacy* (Cambridge/Ma & London, 1989)

M. Hassall and J. Rhodes, 'Excavations at the new Market Hall, Gloucester, 1966-7', *Transactions of the Bristol and Gloucestershire Archaeological Society* 93 (1974) 15-100

M. W. C. Hassall, 'Britain in the *Notitia*', in R. Goodburn and P. Bartholomew (eds), *Aspects of the Notitia Dignitatum*, BAR SS 15 (Oxford, 1976) 103-117

M. Henig, *Religion in Roman Britain* (London, 1984)

M. Henig, 'Souvenir or votive? The Ilam Pan', *ARA: The Bulletin of the Association for Roman Archaeology* 20 (2010/11) 13-5

F. Henry, 'Émailleurs d'occident', *Préhistoire* 2 (1933) 65-146

J. Heurgon, 'The Amiens patera', *Journal of Roman Studies* 41 (1951) 22-24

J. Heurgon, 'La patère d Amiens', *Monuments Piot* 46 (1952a) 93-115

J. Heurgon, 'La fixation des noms de lieux en latin d'après les itinéraires routiers', *Revue de Philologie* 78 (1952b) 169-178

W. Hilgers, *Lateinische Gefässnamen. Bezeichnungen, Funktion und Form römischer Gefässe nach den antiken Schriftquellen*, Bonner Jahrbücher Beihefte 31 (Düsseldorf, 1969)

R. Colt Hoare, *Ancient Wiltshire* I (London, 1812)

N. Hodgson (comp.), *Hadrian's Wall 1999-2009: a summary of excavation and research* (Kendal, 2009)

P. Holder, 'Roman place-names on the Cumbrian Coast', in R. J. A. Wilson and I. D. Caruana (eds), *Romans on the Solway* (Kendal, 2004) 52-65

J. Horsley, *Britannia Romana* (London, 1732)

J. Hughes, 'Hanbury Street, Droitwich: excavations 1980-82', in D. Hurst (ed), *Roman Droitwich* (York, 2006) 46-77

F. Hunter, 'Iron Age hoarding in Scotland and northern England', in A. Gwilt and C. Haselgrove (eds), *Reconstructing Iron Age Societies* (Oxford, 1997) 108-133

F. Hunter, 'The enamelled skillet handle from Ardownie', in S. Anderson, and A. R. Rees, 'The excavation of a large double-chambered souterrain at Ardownie Farm Cottages, Monifieth, Angus', *Tayside & Fife Archaeological Journal* 12 (2006) 28-31

F. Hunter, 'Celtic art in Roman Britain', in D. Garrow, C. Gosden and J. D. Hill (eds), *Rethinking Celtic Art* (Oxford, 2008) 129-45

J. Hunter, *Galloway Byways*, 2nd edn (Dumfries, 2008)

T. Hylton and R. J. Zeepvat, 'Objects of copper alloy, silver and gold', in R. J. Williams and R. J. Zeepvat, *Bancroft. The late Bronze Age and Iron Age settlements and Roman Temple-mausoleum. The Roman villa. Volume II: finds and environmental evidence* (Aylesbury, 1994) 303-21

R. Jackson, 'Waters and spas in the Classical world', in R. S. Porter and W. F. Bynum (eds), *The Medical History of Spas and Waters*, Medical History Supplement no. 10 (1990) 1-13

R. Jackson, 'Spas, waters and hydrotherapy in the Roman world', in J. DeLaine and D. E. Johnston (eds), *Roman Baths and Bathing. Part 1: Bathing and Society*, JRA Supplementary Series No 37 (Portsmouth, Rhode Island, 1999)

R. Jackson, 'Staffordshire Moorlands pan', *British Museum Magazine* 53 (2005) 53

R. Jackson, *Cosmetic Sets of Late Iron Age and Roman Britain*, British Museum Research Publication 181 (London, 2010)

H. James, *Roman Carmarthen: excavations 1978-1993* (London, 2003)

C. Johns, 'An enamelled bronze pyxis from a Roman grave at Elsenham, Essex', *Antiquaries Journal* 73 (1993) 161-165

C. Johns, *The Jewellery of Roman Britain. Celtic and Classical Traditions* (London, 1996)

T. H. Jolliffe, *Archaeology of the Upper Witham Valley*, BAR BS 524 (Oxford, 2010)

G. D. B. Jones and D. J. Woolliscroft, *Hadrian's Wall from the Air* (Stroud, 2001)

E. M. Jope, *Early Celtic Art in the British Isles* (Oxford, 2000)

J. Joy, *Iron Age Mirrors. A biographical approach*, BAR BS 518 (Oxford, 2010)

G. Kabakchieva, 'Set of balsamarium and three strigils', in *The Saved Treasures of Ancient Thrace from the Vassil Bojkov Collection* (Bulgaria, 2009) 184-5

A. Kaufmann-Heinimann, *Götter und Lararien aus Augusta Raurica Herstellung, Fundzusammenhänge und sakrale Function figürlicher Bronzen in einer römischen Stadt*, Forschungen in Augst 26 (1998)

L. Keppie, *The legacy of Rome: Scotland's Roman Remains* (Edinburgh, 2004)

J. R. Kirk, 'Bronzes from Woodeaton, Oxon', *Oxoniensia* 14 (1949) 1-45

A. Koster, *The Bronze Vessels 2. Acquisitions 1954-1996 (including vessels of pewter and iron)* (Nijmegen, 1997)

J. Kunow, 'Zum Analphabetentum im römischen Heer – Angaben von Lebensalter und Dienstzeit auf Grabsteinen der Provinz Germania inferior', *Archäologisches Korrespondenzblatt* 13 (1983) 483-485

E. Künzl, 'Großformatige Emailobjekte der römischen Kaiserzeit', in S. T. A. M. Mols, A. M. Gerhartl-Witteveen, H. Kars, A. Koster, E. J. T. Peters and W. J. H. Willems (eds), *Acta of the 12th International Congress on Ancient Bronzes, Nijmegen 1992* (Nijmegen, 1995) 39-49

E. Künzl, 'Enamelled bronzes from Roman Britain: Celtic art and tourist knick-knacks', *Current Archaeology* 222 (2008) 22-27

E. Künzl, 'Celtic craftsmanship and Roman etiquette', in F. Müller (ed), *Art of the Celts 700 BC to AD 700* (Berne, 2009) 254-55

E. Künzl and G. Koeppel, 'Souvenirs und Devotionalien. Zeugnisse des geschäftlichen, religiösen und kulturellen Tourismus im antiken Römerreich', *Sonderband Antike Welt*. Zaberns Bildbände zur Archäologie (Mainz, 2002)

S. Künzl, 'Ein griechisches Goldmedaillon aus Makedonien', *Jahrbuch RGZM* 47 (2000) 329-335

A. M. Leskow, W. L. Lapuschnjan and W. A. Nabatschikow, *Gold und Kunsthandwerk vom antiken Kuban, Neue archäologische Entdeckungen aus der Sowjetunion* (Stuttgart, 1989)

J. Liversidge, *Britain in the Roman Empire* (London, 1968)

G. Lloyd-Morgan, 'Discussion', in D. F. Mackreth, 'Personal Ornaments', in J. Hughes, 'Hanbury Street, Droitwich: excavations 1980-82', in D. Hurst (ed), *Roman Droitwich* (York, 2006) 66-7

U. Lund Hansen, *Römischer Import im Norden* (Copenhagen, 1987)

L'or des Scythes, *Trésors de l'Ermitage* (Bruxelles, 1991)

M. R. McCarthy, *A Roman, Anglian and Medieval Site at Blackfriars Street, Carlisle: excavations 1977-9* (Kendal, 1990)

P. Macdonald, *Llyn Cerrig Bach: a study of the copper alloy artefacts from the insular La Tène assemblage* (Cardiff, 2007a)

P. Macdonald, 'Perspectives on insular La Tène art', in C. C. Haselgrove & T. Moore (ed), *The Later Iron Age in Britain and Beyond* (Oxford, 2007b) 329-38

M. MacGregor, *Early Celtic Art in North Britain* (Leicester, 1976)

N. Mahéo, *Les Collections Archéologiques du Musée de Picardie* (Amiens, 1990)

J. C. Mann, 'Birdoswald to Ravenglass', *Britannia* 20 (1989) 75-79

P. Masser and J. Evans, 'Excavations within the vicus settlement at Burgh by Sands, 2002', *CW*³ 5 (2005) 31-63

R. Megaw and V. Megaw, *Celtic art: from its beginnings to the Book of Kells*, 2nd edn (London, 2001)

H. Menzel, *Die römischen Bronzen aus Deutschland 3, Bonn* (Mainz, 1986)

C. N. Moore, 'An enamelled skillet-handle from Brough-on-Fosse and the distribution of similar vessels', *Britannia* 9 (1978) 319-27

B. N. Mozolevskij, *Tovsta Mogila* (Kiev, 1979)

F. Müller, *Götter, Gaben, Rituale. Religion in der Frühgeschichte Europas* (Mainz, 2002)

M. Pitts and S. Worrell, 'Dish fit for the gods', *British Archaeology* 73 (2003) 22-27

T. W. Potter, *Roman Britain* (London, 1983)

T. Potter and C. Johns, *Roman Britain* (London, 1992)

RCAHMS *Tenth Report with Inventory of Monuments and Constructions in the Counties of Midlothian and West Lothian* (Edinburgh, 1929)

I. A. Richmond and O. G. S. Crawford, 'The British Section of the Ravenna Cosmography', *Archaeologia* 93 (1949) 11-50

A. L. F. Rivet and C. Smith, *The Place-Names of Roman Britain* (London, 1979)

A. S. Robertson, 'Roman finds from non-Roman sites in Scotland', *Britannia* 1 (1970) 198-226.

A. Rogerson, 'Excavations at Scole, 1973', *East Anglian Archaeology* 5 (1977) 97-224

M. C. Ross, 'Byzantine Bronze Peacock Lamps', *Archaeology* 13 (1960) 134-6

M. Roxan, 'Veteran settlement of the auxilia in Germania', in G. Alföldy, B. Dobson and W. Eck (eds), *Kaiser, Heer und Gesellschaft in der Römischen Kaiserzeit* (Stuttgart, 2000) 307-26

J. Schnetz, *Itineraria Romana, vol. II: Ravennatis Anonymi Cosmographia et Guidonis Geographica* (Stuttgart, 1942; reprinted 1990)

R. A. Smith, *British Museum Guide to Roman Britain* (London, 1922)

I. M. Stead, Celtic *Art in Britain before the Roman Conquest* (London, 1985)

I. M. Stead and K. Hughes, *Early Celtic Designs* (London, 1997)

D. E. Strong, *Greek and Roman Gold and Silver Plate* (London, 1966)

W. Stukeley, *Itinerarium Curiosus* (London, 1776)

W.-R. Teegen, 'Studien zu dem kaiserzeitlichen Quellopferfund von Bad Pyrmont', *Ergänzungsband zum Reallexikon der Germanischen Altertumskunde* 20 (Berlin, 1999)

R. S. O. Tomlin, 'Inscriptions on metal vessels' in B. Cunliffe 1988, 55-7

R. S. O. Tomlin, 'Roman Britain in 2010 III. Inscriptions', *Britannia* 42 (2011) 439-66

R. S. O. Tomlin and M. W. C. Hassall, 'Roman Britain in 2003 III. Inscriptions', *Britannia* 35 (2004) 335-349

Trésors archéologiques du Nord de la France, Musée des Beaux-Arts de Valenciennes (Valenciennes, 1997)

J. M. C. Toynbee, *Art in Roman Britain* (London, 1962)

A. Trotter, *East Galloway Sketches* (Castle Douglas, 1901)

M. True and K. Hamma (eds), *A Passion for Antiquities: ancient art from the collection of Barbara and Lawrence Fleischman* (Malibu, 1994)

F. Vasselle, 'Compte rendu des trouvailles faites à Amiens en 1948 et 1949', *Bulletin de la Société des Antiquaires de Picardie* 43 (1949-50) 226-40

M. Vermeulen-Bekkering, Transformations. Germania Inferior. Development of cult: Gods, http://www2.rgzm.de/transformation/home/FramesUK.cfm (Accessed March 2011)

A. Way, 'Proceedings of meetings, May 1, 1837', *Archaeological Journal* (1857) 282-4

A. Way, *Catalogue of Antiquities, Works of Art and Historical Scottish Relics exhibited in the Museum of the Archaeological Institute of Great Britain and Ireland during their Annual Meeting at Edinburgh, July 1856* (Edinburgh/London, 1859)

G. Webster, 'Bronze (copper alloy), silver and gold', in R. Turner, *Excavations of an Iron Age Settlement and Roman Religious Complex at Ivy Chimneys, Witham, Essex 1978-83 = East Anglian Archaeology* 88 (1999) 79-96

R. J. A. Wilson and I. Caruana, *Romans on the Solway. Essays in Honour of Richard Bellhouse*. Cumberland and Westmorland Antiquarian and Archaeological Society, Extra series 21 (Kendal, 2004)

S. Worrell, 'Roman Britain in 2003. II. Finds Reported under the Portable Antiquities Scheme', *Britannia* 35 (2004) 317-334

S. Worrell, 'Roman Britain in 2005. II. Finds Reported under the Portable Antiquities Scheme', *Britannia* 37 (2006) 429-466

S. Worrell, 'Roman Britain in 2008. II. Finds Reported under the Portable Antiquities Scheme', *Britannia* 40 (2009) 281-312

S. Worrell and J. Pearce, 'Roman Britain in 2010. II. Finds reported under the Portable Antiquities Scheme', *Brittania* 42 (2011) 399-437

A. N. Zadoks-Josephus, J. Jitta, W. J. T. Peters and W. A. van Es, *Roman Bronze Statuettes from the Netherlands I, Scripta Archaeologica Groningana* 1 (Groningen, 1967)

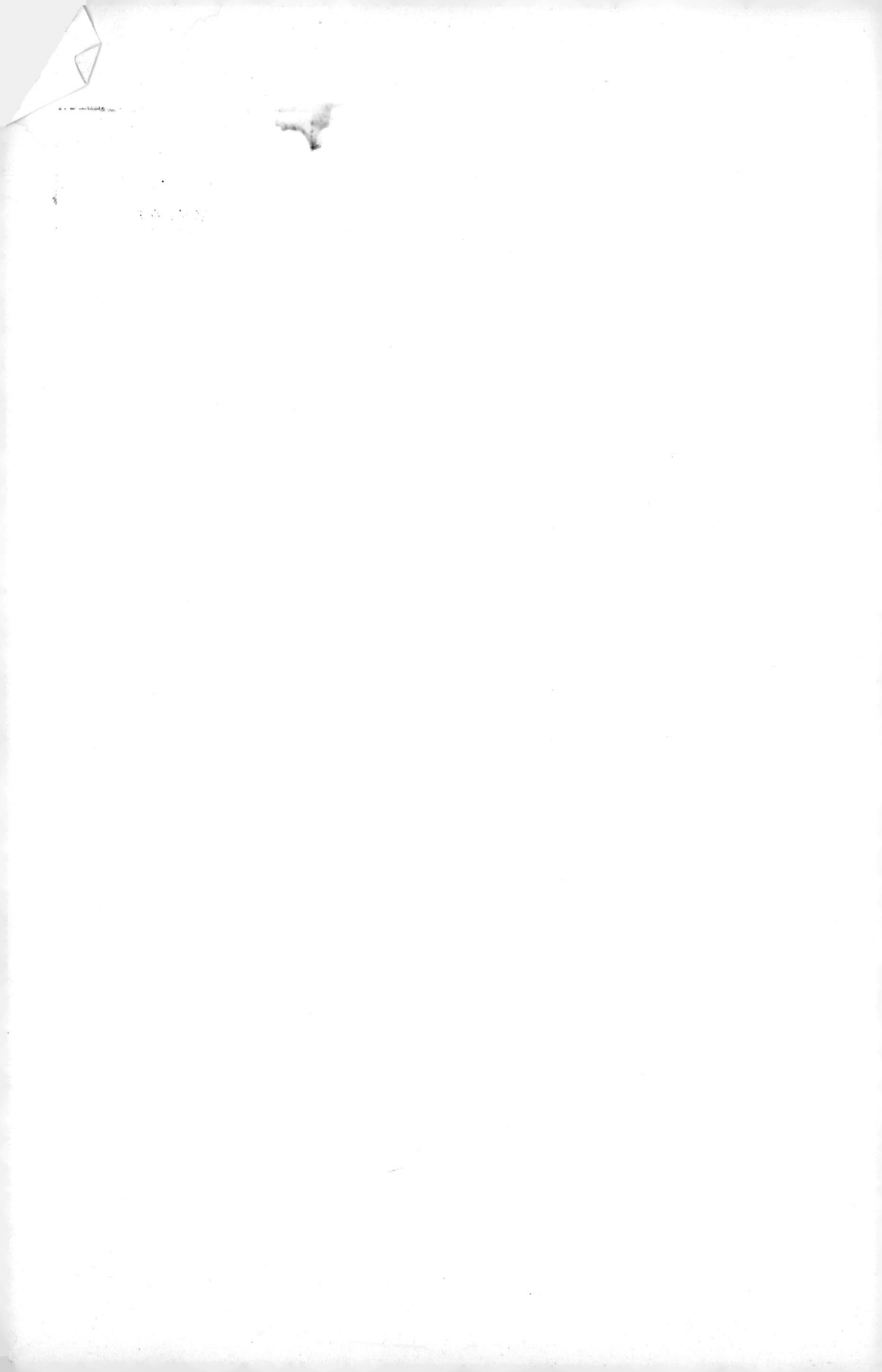